Dodd-Frank

Dodd-Frank

What It Does and Why It's Flawed

edited by Hester Peirce and James Broughel

MERCATUS CENTER
George Mason University

Arlington, Virginia

About the Mercatus Center at George Mason University

The Mercatus Center at George Mason University is the world's premier university source for market-oriented ideas—bridging the gap between academic ideas and real-world problems.

A university-based research center, Mercatus advances knowledge about how markets work to improve people's lives by training graduate students, conducting research, and applying economics to offer solutions to society's most pressing problems.

Our mission is to generate knowledge and understanding of the institutions that affect the freedom to prosper and to find sustainable solutions that overcome the barriers preventing individuals from living free, prosperous, and peaceful lives.

Founded in 1980, the Mercatus Center is located on George Mason University's Arlington campus.

www.mercatus.org

Copyright © 2012 by James Broughel, Robert W. Greene, Patrick A. McLaughlin, Hester Peirce, J. W. Verret, Lawrence J. White, and the Mercatus Center at George Mason University

Mercatus Center
George Mason University
3351 N. Fairfax Drive
Arlington, VA 22201

Typeset by Sidecar Studio, Harrisonburg, Virginia. Composed in Veronika Burian and José Scaglione's Abril.

Library of Congress Cataloging-in-Publication Data

Dodd-Frank : what it does and why it's flawed / edited by Hester Peirce
and James Broughel.
     pages cm.
   Includes index.
   ISBN 978-0-9836077-7-9 (pbk.) -- ISBN 978-0-9836077-8-6 (e-book)
   1. United States. Dodd-Frank Wall Street Reform and Consumer Protection
Act. 2. Financial services industry--Law and legislation--United States.
3. Financial institutions--Law and legislation--United States. I.
Peirce, Hester, editor. II. Broughel, James, 1981- editor.
   KF969.58201.A2 2013
   346.73'082--dc23
                    2012051429

First published, December 2012
Printed in the United States of America

Contents

"In the economic sphere an act, a habit, an institution, a law produces not only one effect, but a series of effects. Of these effects, the first alone is immediate; it appears simultaneously with its cause; it is seen. The other effects emerge only subsequently; they are not seen; we are fortunate if we foresee them."

—Frédéric Bastiat, "What Is Seen and Not Seen" (1850)

"One of the great mistakes is to judge policies and programs by their intentions rather than their results."

—Milton Friedman, in a 1975 interview with Richard Heffner on *The Open Mind*

Introduction

by Hester Peirce and James Broughel

I T HAS BEEN more than five years since the financial crisis began and more than two years since the passage of the legislative response, the Dodd-Frank Wall Street Reform and Consumer Protection Act (Dodd-Frank).[1] The nature and magnitude of the effects of the largest piece of financial legislation in generations will become clearer as regulators exercise the broad discretion given them under the act. Regulators' efforts at implementation are far from complete, with many of the rules still unwritten and others not yet in effect. Regardless of how the rules are written, the act will certainly have far-reaching effects on the financial system and our economy. This book takes the opportunity to look at Dodd-Frank as it is being implemented and asks whether it is an effective response to the financial crisis that so deeply rattled our nation.

As is typical of crisis legislation, Dodd-Frank included many provisions crafted in haste and many other provisions drafted before the crisis for which the act provided a convenient legislative vehicle. Even as the law was being passed, its proponents acknowledged its imperfections.[2] In the years since the law's passage, the fundamental flaws with the legislation have become more evident.[3] Dodd-Frank not only failed effectively and holistically to respond to the crisis, but it also gives rise to a whole new set of problems that could overshadow the act's good elements and lay the groundwork for a future financial crisis.

Many of the provisions in Dodd-Frank are entirely unrelated to the crisis. Title IV, which requires hedge-fund registration, and Title XV, which imposes a number of miscellaneous disclosure provisions on public companies, illustrate this phenomenon. Another example is the "Durbin amendment" in Title X, which sets price controls on fees banks can charge merchants in connection with debit cards.

Other provisions, while purportedly solutions to real problems that emerged in the crisis, could serve to exacerbate those problems. As one example, Lawrence J. White explains in his essay in part II how Title IX's regulatory regime for credit rating agencies will decrease competition and thus solidify the market share of the largest credit rating agencies.

The most striking omission of the act was its failure even to attempt to reform the broken housing-finance system in the United States. The legislation ignored Fannie Mae and Freddie Mac, the flawed government-sponsored mortgage giants at the heart of the housing crisis. White explains the gravity of this omission and Congress's continuing failure to act with respect to housing-finance reform. The failure to act is not for want of workable solutions,[4] but is a result of the interest special-interest groups have in maintaining the status quo.

Dodd-Frank's proponents portray it as a solution to the too-big-to-fail problem that led to the massive bailouts during the financial crisis. A closer look at Dodd-Frank suggests that it not only failed to solve the too-big-to fail problem, but it also institutionalized the problem. One of Dodd-Frank's new bureaucracies, the Financial Stability Oversight Council (FSOC), has new power to designate firms "systemically important," a phrase even experts on macroprudential regulation have trouble defining in an agreed-upon way.[5] White points out that these designated firms will receive special regulatory treatment. As the Title I section describes, the additional regulatory burden will be accompanied by an unspoken commitment that regulators will step in to save designated firms and their creditors if there is trouble. This implicit government guarantee carries a perverse incentive for large firms to take on more risk and a decreased incentive for large firms' shareholders and counterparties to penalize them for doing so.

Also contributing to the institutionalization of too-big-to-fail is the concentration of risk that emerges from Dodd-Frank. As the Title VII section discusses, derivatives clearinghouses after Dodd-Frank will form a new set of large, interconnected, critically important financial entities. Likewise, the government's involvement in the mortgage market has grown after the financial crisis, and Dodd-Frank's securitization reforms solidify the continued dominance of taxpayer-supported housing finance.

The companion of Dodd-Frank's entrenchment of big financial companies is its adverse effect on small ones. With its numerous and incomprehensible complexities, Dodd-Frank gives big banks a competitive edge over their smaller rivals, who are less able to hire the lawyers and compliance personnel necessary to advise on complying with the law in the most cost-effective manner. The effects on small banks may be one of the most profound unintended consequences of a law designed to rein in big banks, but only time will tell.

Dodd-Frank creates a regulatory system that suppresses market discipline in favor of regulatory expertise and broad regulatory authority. Congress left key decisions to regulators; it afforded them tremendous discretion to define the limits of their own authority and places unrealistic expectations upon them.[6] The underlying assumption that regulators can effectively micromanage the market is flawed.[7] Giving regulators more levers to pull and buttons to push with respect to the financial system only creates a false sense of security.

The irony of expanding the role of regulators in the aftermath of a financial crisis in which regulators were complicit is heightened by the fact that even failed regulators were given new powers. With the exception of the Office of Thrift Supervision, which was eliminated, regulators were not held accountable for regulatory failures but were rewarded with new powers. The sections on Titles I, VIII, and IX, for example, discuss some of the new powers given to the Securities and Exchange Commission (SEC) and to the Federal Reserve (Fed), both of which failed quite dramatically in their oversight roles the last time around. In the case of the Fed, as the Title XI section details, Dodd-Frank introduced some new transparency and accountability mechanisms for its future bailout programs. Nevertheless, questions remain about the adequacy of these reforms.

To make matters worse, Dodd-Frank gives some of these regulators a free hand, with few meaningful accountability checks, to intervene in the economy as they please. For example, Title II authorizes the Federal Deposit Insurance Corporation (FDIC) to take over and liquidate companies, and Title X creates the remarkably unaccountable Consumer Financial Protection Bureau (CFPB) within the Fed.

The CFPB is one of the powerful new bureaucracies created by Dodd-Frank. The FSOC and the Office of Financial Research (OFR) are two other new Dodd-Frank agencies. As the sections on Titles I and X discuss, these agencies are shielded from accountability to Congress, the president, and the American people.

So much of the decision making was left to regulators that the full implications of the law may not be known for years. The implementation process is not keeping pace with statutory requirements, and many deadlines have been missed.[8] Implementing the vague concepts laid out in Dodd-Frank is not an easy task, as the Volcker Rule discussion in White's essay and the Title VI section illustrate. Most Dodd-Frank rules are being crafted without the benefit of thorough economic analysis.[9] The rulemaking gaps and absence of economic analysis mean market participants and regulators remain uncertain about how Dodd-Frank will work in practice. As one example, regulators only recently defined a derivative, though that definition is central to all of the derivatives reforms in Title VII of the act.[10]

Adverse consequences for consumers are already coming to light. As is often the case, measures intended to protect consumers can end up harming them. Given Dodd-Frank's breadth, these consequences range from possible threats to privacy, as discussed in the Title I section, to decreased consumer choice and increased consumer costs, as discussed in the Title X and XIV sections. The Title XIV section provides an example of a troubling trend in regulatory policy—the idea that government knows better than consumers what is best for them. Government officials have taken on the paternalistic role of safely steering citizens toward "better" or "safer" products and services. As a consequence, consumers increasingly will face a one-size-fits-all market that costs more and offers fewer choices.

Another less obvious ramification of Dodd-Frank is that it distracts regulators from their core missions. The Title IV section discusses this phenomenon in the context of the SEC's new hedge-fund authorities. Likewise, the Commodity Futures Trading Commission (CFTC), newly preoccupied with regulating systemic risk,[11] has found it difficult to devote adequate time to handling the recent failures of two CFTC-regulated firms that resulted in substantial retail customer losses.

Many of the consequences of Dodd-Frank remain to be seen, but as McLaughlin and Greene demonstrate in their essay in Part II, Dodd-Frank already has had a measurable effect. Using the content of the regulatory text itself as a data source, they quantify the number of new restrictions generated by Dodd-Frank rules in 2010 and 2011. If the new Dodd-Frank rules create restrictions at the same rate, the authors estimate that Dodd-Frank will cause a 26 percent increase in the number of restrictions in the financial market regulation titles of the Code of Federal Regulations.

Often it is suggested that although Dodd-Frank has its problems, no other solutions were being proposed at the time. As J. W.

Verret demonstrates in his essay in part II, there were other ideas for remaking the financial regulatory system. Verret discusses then–Treasury Secretary Henry Paulson's blueprint for financial reform, which came out in early 2008. Although that plan also had weaknesses, some of the suggested reforms proved prescient, such as recommended mortgage-market reforms. The blueprint recommended merging the CFTC and the SEC, agencies with considerable regulatory overlap. Dodd-Frank not only fails to implement this idea, but, as the Title VII section illustrates, it also gives the agencies redundant rule-writing tasks related to derivatives. Verret shows that although the Paulson plan was not perfect, its existence demonstrates that alternative paths for financial reform could have been considered.

This book is not intended to provide a comprehensive summary of Dodd-Frank, but rather it seeks to offer a closer look at some of its provisions in an effort to seriously assess its efficacy. Looking behind the act's celebrated objectives shows that it not only fails to achieve many of its stated goals, but it also reinforces dangerous regulatory pathologies that became evident during the last crisis and creates new pathologies that could lay the groundwork for the next crisis.

NOTES

1. *Dodd-Frank Wall Street Reform and Consumer Protection Act,* Public Law 111-203, *U.S. Statutes at Large* 124 (2010), 1376.

2. See, for example, Jim Kuhnhenn, "Congress Approves Sweeping Reforms," *Bloomberg BusinessWeek,* July 15, 2010, http://www.businessweek.com/ap/financial news/D9GVN38O1.htm. The article quotes Senator Dodd shortly after the passage of the bill, saying, "It is not a perfect bill, I will be the first to admit that. . . . It will take the next economic crisis, as certainly it will come, to determine whether or not the provisions of this bill will actually provide this generation or the next generation of regulators with the tools necessary to minimize the effects of that crisis."

3. See, for example, "Dodd-Frank's Financial Outsourcing," *Wall Street Journal,*

November 6, 2012. The editorial notes that Dodd-Frank "is producing an amazing trifecta: anger among our international trading partners, a less prosperous financial market at home, and a larger taxpayer safety net."

4. See, for example, Lawrence J. White, "The Way Forward: U.S. Residential–Mortgage Finance in a Post-GSE World," in *House of Cards: Reforming America's Housing Finance System,* ed. Satya Thallam (Arlington, VA: Mercatus Center at George Mason University, March 2012), 67, http://mercatus.org/publication/house-cards.

5. See David VanHoose, "Systemic Risks and Macroprudential Regulation: A Critical Appraisal" (Networks Financial Institute Policy Brief 2011-PB-04, Indiana State University, Terre Haute, IN, April 2011), http://papers.ssrn.com/sol3/papers.cfm?abstract_id=1816476&download=yes.

6. Senator Ted Kaufman, who voted for the legislation, made this point: "Congress largely has decided instead to punt decisions to the regulators, saddling them with a mountain of rule-makings and studies." Quoted in Jim Kuhnhenn, "Congress Approves Sweeping Reforms."

7. Hayek warned of the impossibility of any "single brain" mastering the information necessary to run a market and cautioned against efforts to micromanage "the market and similar social structures":

> The recognition of the insuperable limits to his knowledge ought indeed to teach the student of society a lesson of humility which should guard him against becoming an accomplice in men's fatal striving to control society—a striving which makes him not only a tyrant over his fellows, but which may well make him the destroyer of a civilization which no brain has designed but which has grown from the free efforts of millions of individuals.

Friedrich August von Hayek, "The Pretence of Knowledge" (Nobel Prize lecture, Royal Swedish Academy of Sciences, Stockholm, Sweden, December 11, 1974), http://www.nobelprize.org/nobel_prizes/economics/laureates/1974/hayek-lecture.html.

8. As of November 1, 2012, of the 237 rulemaking deadlines that had passed, 61 percent had been missed. Davis Polk, "Dodd-Frank Progress Report," Davis Polk Regulatory Tracker, November 2012, 2, http://www.davispolk.com/files/Publication/9a990de9-911b-4e6b-b183-08b071d8b008/Presentation/PublicationAttachment/8363256a-524d-4d65-8ebe-096127dab2a3/Nov2012_Dodd.Frank.Progress.Report.pdf.

9. Committee on Capital Markets Regulation (CCMR), "CCMR Warns That Inadequate Cost-Benefit Analysis Opens Dodd-Frank Rulemaking to Challenge and Delay," news release, March 7, 2012, http://capmktsreg.org/pdfs/2012.03.07_CBA_let

ter.pdf. A letter to several congressional committee members is included in the release. It reports results of an analysis of 192 Dodd-Frank rulemakings, the vast majority of which were conducted without thorough cost-benefit analysis. See also Hester Peirce, "Economic Analysis by Federal Financial Regulators" (working paper 12-131, Mercatus Center at George Mason University, Arlington, VA, October 2012), http://mercatus.org/sites/default/files/FinancialRegulators_Peirce_v1-0_1 .pdf.

10. Commodity Futures Trading Commission (CFTC) and SEC, "Further Definition of 'Swap,' 'Security-Based Swap,' and 'Security-Based Swap Agreement'; Mixed Swaps; Security-Based Swap Agreement Recordkeeping," Notice of Final Rulemaking, *Federal Register* 77 (August 13, 2012).

11. According to the CFTC's website, the CFTC's new "mission is to protect market users and the public from fraud, manipulation, abusive practices and systemic risk related to derivatives, and to foster open, competitive, and financially sound markets." See CFTC, "Missions and Responsibilities," http://www.cftc.gov/About/Mis sionResponsibilities/index.htm.

Abbreviations

CFPB	Consumer Financial Protection Bureau
CFTC	Commodity Futures Trading Commission
CFR	Code of Federal Regulations
CPFF	Commercial Paper Funding Facility
DIF	Deposit Insurance Fund
DRC	Democratic Republic of the Congo
E&S	examinable and supervisable
FDIC	Federal Deposit Insurance Corporation
Fed	Federal Reserve
FHA	Federal Housing Administration
FHFA	Federal Housing Finance Agency
FIO	Federal Insurance Office
FOIA	Freedom of Information Act
FRA	Federal Reserve Act
FSOC	Financial Stability Oversight Council
GAO	Government Accountability Office
GSE	government-sponsored enterprise
HUD	Department of Housing and Urban Development
ICE	IntercontinentalExchange
ILC	industrial loan company
MBS	mortgage-backed securities
MSRB	Municipal Securities Rulemaking Board
NRSRO	nationally recognized statistical rating organization
OCC	Office of the Comptroller of the Currency
OFR	Office of Financial Research
OLA	Orderly Liquidation Authority
OTC	over-the-counter
OTS	Office of Thrift Supervision
PWG	President's Working Group
QRM	Qualified Residential Mortgage

Abbreviations

RFC	Reconstruction Finance Corporation
SDR	Swap-Data Repository
SEC	Securities and Exchange Commission
SEF	Swap Execution Facility
SIFI	systemically important financial institution
TALF	Term Asset-Backed Securities Loan Facility
TARP	Troubled Asset Relief Program
USAID	United States Agency for International Development

PART I
A Title-by-Title Look at Dodd-Frank

by Hester Peirce

The country suffered a terrible financial crisis. It started in 2007, and its reverberations continue to affect the real economy and financial sector five years later. Dodd-Frank was the legislative response to that crisis. This chapter provides a window into each title of Dodd-Frank in an effort to assess whether its provisions support the claim that the act provides a solution to the problems that led to the financial crisis. Too often the purported solutions threaten to become the source of new problems in the financial sector, consumer pocketbooks, and the economy as a whole.

What Title I does:

Title I establishes the Financial Stability Oversight Council (FSOC), a multiregulator systemic-risk council.

It establishes the Office of Financial Research (OFR), an office to collect, disseminate, and study financial data.

It identifies systemically important financial institutions for special regulation by the Federal Reserve (Fed).

It requires regulators to impose enhanced capital requirements and leverage limits.

Why Title I's approach is flawed:

FSOC has not played an effective coordinating role in the crucial initial years of regulatory implementation of Dodd-Frank.

Designating specific firms as systemically important creates a market expectation that designated firms are too big to fail and thus dulls market discipline.

The Fed's bank-centric regulatory model will not work for nonbanks.

The structure of the OFR enables it to operate without the accountability expected to apply to government agencies and without adequate safeguards on data.

TITLE I

Financial Stability

T ITLE I OF Dodd-Frank is intended to enhance financial stability. To achieve this end, it establishes two new government entities, the Financial Stability Oversight Council (FSOC) and the Office of Financial Research (OFR). Although each agency has a commendable mission at first glance, each is fundamentally flawed.

The FSOC is a multiregulator council intended to take a broad view of the financial system and identify emerging systemic risks.[1] It brings the nation's financial regulators together to identify and respond to risks to the financial stability of the United States. As Treasury Secretary Timothy Geithner has acknowledged implicitly, however, that mission is somewhat futile. He warned that "we cannot predict the precise threats that may face the financial system"[2] and cautioned that "you won't be able to make a judgment about what's systemic and what's not until you know the nature of the shock."[3] Worse than being ineffective, the FSOC could have harmful effects on the financial system.[4]

The FSOC has struggled to fulfill even some of the more concrete tasks Dodd-Frank assigned. For example, one of its statutory mandates is facilitating coordination among member agencies. A lack of coordination has marked the Dodd-Frank implementation process, perhaps illustrated most dramatically by the Commodity Futures Trading Commission (CFTC) decision to issue its own Volcker Rule proposal months after the other financial regulators responsible for the rule issued a joint proposal.[5] The FSOC has failed to think about how the package of regulations being implemented by the different regulators works together and the aggregate costs and benefits it will generate. This lack of coordination has added a layer of complexity to an already complex Dodd-Frank rulemaking process. The FSOC has not used its authority to play a valuable coordinating role.[6]

One of the key Dodd-Frank mandates for the FSOC is the identification of nonbank financial companies that are systemically important and require special oversight by the Federal Reserve (Fed). The FSOC is currently in the process of determining which companies should be designated.[7] In considering whether a company qualifies, Dodd-Frank tells the FSOC to consider whether material financial distress at the company or the nature, scope, size, scale, concentration, or mix of the company's activities could pose a threat to the financial stability of the United States.

Singling out a group of entities in this manner directly conflicts with one of the statutory purposes of the FSOC: "To promote market discipline, by eliminating expectations on the part of shareholders, creditors, and counterparties of [large, interconnected] companies that the Government will shield them from losses in the event of failure."[8] Companies designated by the FSOC will be perceived as too big to fail.[9] Shareholders, creditors, and counterparties will assume that the government will step in if there is a problem at one of these entities and, accordingly, will exercise less due diligence of their own. The resulting diminution of scrutiny by other market participants will make it easier for a firm to take risks for which it is undercompensated and unhedged and to engage in destabilizing activities. Shareholders, creditors, and taxpayers could be exposed to greater losses than they would have been exposed to if market participants monitored firms more closely.

Dodd-Frank tries to compensate for this diminished market discipline by relying on more stringent regulation. Entities designated by the FSOC will be subject to an additional layer of regulation by the Fed, including more stringent capital requirements and leverage limits.[10] For example, designated nonbank financial companies and large bank holding companies have to submit resolution plans to the Fed and the Federal Deposit Insurance Corporation (FDIC), are subject—along with their subsidiaries—to examination by the Fed, may be forced to divest certain assets, have to obtain preapproval for certain acquisitions, will be subject to enhanced prudential standards (including graduated risk-based capital requirements, liquidity requirements, and concentration limits), and may be subject to remediation requirements in the event of financial distress.[11]

As we saw in the last crisis, regulators often miss problems at the companies they regulate. The task of overseeing nonbank financial companies takes the Fed outside its area of expertise, which has centered on banks and bank holding companies. The requirements imposed on nonbank financial companies are likely to be ill-suited to their unique characteristics. Existing regulators may pay less attention to the subsidiaries they regulate, with the expectation that the Fed is regulating the whole company.[12] Under the Dodd-Frank regime, regulatory failures could be more likely than before.

If a designated firm runs into trouble, the Fed, in order to protect its own reputation, will have an incentive to prevent the firm's problems from becoming publicly known. A firm's failure (or rumors of its potential failure) to pay its creditors or counterparties would reflect badly on the Fed as a regulator. As a consequence, regulators can be expected to intervene to keep these companies afloat.[13] These companies will be perceived as better credit risks than other companies, and their cost of funding will be lower. Normal market processes by which firms come and go over time will be impeded.

The fact that many companies have argued against designation reflects an uncertainty about the costs the new regulatory structure will impose and a fear of the up-front costs.[14] Initial costs undoubtedly will be high as the new regulatory structure is developed and tailored for nonbank financial companies. Dodd-Frank gives designated firms a chance to challenge the designation, and some firms likely will avail themselves of this option.

A firm that is designated and then successfully challenges the designation in court would be able to avoid the extra regulatory costs while still enjoying the market's recognition that regulators think the firm is too big to fail. A successful challenge will be hard given the short window of time (30 days after designation) for mounting a challenge and the fact that judicial review is limited to consideration of whether the final determination was arbitrary and capricious.[15] Nevertheless, the possibility of obtaining the aura of a designation without the concomitant costs of additional regulation will make challenges likely.

The second new entity created by Dodd-Frank is the OFR, the mission of which is to assist the FSOC and its member agencies. The OFR might play a useful role in helping to standardize data collections by the federal financial regulators and helping to eliminate duplicative reporting. The legislative mandate and structure of the OFR, however, enables it to operate without the meaningful accountability that we expect to apply to government agencies.

Although the OFR is an office within the Treasury, it enjoys nearly complete autonomy. Its single director is nominated by the president and confirmed by the Senate.[16] The director has a six-year term, and Dodd-Frank does not give the president any grounds for removing him. The director must report annually to Congress on the activities of the OFR but is not otherwise accountable to Congress.

After consulting with the Treasury secretary,[17] the director determines the OFR's budget, which is funded by an assessment on large bank holding companies and nonbank financial companies supervised by the Fed.[18] The OFR possesses subpoena power to obtain data from financial companies. The OFR's mandate to assist the FSOC in carrying out its systemic-oversight functions makes it likely that the OFR will seek to collect a broad array of data. Likewise, fear of being faulted for missing a future crisis militates for extensive data collection.

In addition to collecting data, the OFR will disseminate it. Dodd-Frank ambiguously directs the OFR to

> provide certain data to financial industry participants and to the general public to increase market transparency and facilitate research on the financial system, to the extent that intellectual property rights are not violated, business confidential information is properly protected, and the sharing of such information poses no significant threats to the financial system of the United States.[19]

This broad directive to share information widely—with only passing mention of protecting "business confidential information" and without specific mention of the protection of personal financial information—is troubling. Given that consumer mortgage transactions were at the heart of the last financial crisis, the OFR is likely to seek consumer-level data. Particularly because the OFR has a mandate to disseminate data, Dodd-Frank should have included more explicit protections for confidential information.

Title I was an attempt to respond to the financial crisis, but it did so in a way that delegates vast authority to regulators and helps lay the groundwork for another crisis or for future bailouts of companies identified by the government as too important to fail. Increased regulatory coordination and better access to information about the financial markets are important, but more stringent, more encompassing regulation is not a substitute for market discipline inspired by the real fear of losing money without a government backstop.

Title I undermines, rather than encourages, this type of market discipline. The FSOC's designation of entities sends the signal to the market that there is a subset of entities that will not be allowed to fail. Market participants will feel they do not need to exercise the same level of diligence with respect to these entities as they do with respect to others.

NOTES

1. The FSOC's voting members are the Treasury secretary, the Federal Reserve chairman, the comptroller of the currency, the director of the Consumer Financial Protection Bureau, the chairman of the Securities and Exchange Commission, the chairman of the Federal Deposit Insurance Corporation, the chairman of the Commodity Futures Trading Commission (CFTC), the director of the Federal Housing Finance Agency, the chairman of the National Credit Union Administration Board, and a presidentially appointed insurance expert. The FSOC's nonvoting members are the director of the Office of Financial Research, the director of the Federal Insurance Office, a state insurance commissioner, a state banking supervisor, and a state securities commissioner.

2. Timothy F. Geithner, "Letter from the Chair," in *2011 FSOC Annual Report to Congress* (Washington, DC: FSOC, 2011), ii, http://www.treasury.gov/initiatives/fsoc /Documents/Letter%20from%20the%20Chair.pdf.

3. Special Inspector General for the Troubled Asset Relief Program (SIGTARP), "Audit Report: Extraordinary Relief Provided to Citigroup, Inc." (SIGTARP-11-002, Washington, DC, January 13, 2011), 43 (quoting Secretary Geithner), http://www .sigtarp.gov/Audit%20Reports/Extraordinary%20Financial%20Assistance%20 Provided%20to%20Citigroup,%20Inc.pdf.

4. See David VanHoose, "Systemic Risks and Macroprudential Regulation: A Critical Appraisal" (Networks Financial Institute Policy Brief 2011-PB-04, Indiana State University, Terre Haute, IN, April 2011), http://papers.ssrn.com/sol3/papers.cfm ?abstract_id=1816476&download=yes. VanHoose points out drawbacks of the new macroprudential regulatory layer, including increased opportunity for regulatory capture and further displacement of market discipline.

5. CFTC, "Prohibitions and Restrictions on Proprietary Trading and Certain Interests in, and Relationships with, Hedge Funds and Covered Funds," Notice of Proposed Rulemaking, *Federal Register* 77 (February 14, 2012), 8332; OCC et al.,

"Prohibitions and Restrictions on Proprietary Trading and Certain Interests in, and Relationships with, Hedge Funds and Private Equity Funds," Notice of Proposed Rulemaking, *Federal Register* 76 (November 7, 2011), 68846.

6. See, for example, Government Accountability Office, "New Council and Research Office Should Strengthen Their Accountability and Transparency of Their Decisions" (GAO 12-866, Washington, DC, September 2012), 55. Based on a finding that the FSOC has not fulfilled its coordinating role adequately to date, the GAO calls on the FSOC to "establish formal collaboration and coordination policies that clarify issues such as when collaboration or coordination should occur and what role FSOC should play in facilitating that coordination."

7. In April, the FSOC issued a final rule and interpretive guidance related to the designation of nonbank financial companies. FSOC, "Authority to Require Supervision and Regulation of Certain Nonbank Financial Companies," Final Rule and Interpretive Guidance, *Federal Register* 77 (April 11, 2012), 21637.

8. *Dodd-Frank Wall Street Reform and Consumer Protection Act,* Public Law 111-203, *U.S. Statutes at Large* 124 (2010), § 112(a)(1)(B).

9. Large financial institutions that became bank holding companies during the crisis, that received Troubled Asset Relief Program (TARP) funds during the crisis, and that abandon their bank holding company status will be treated as if they had been designated by the FSOC. *Dodd-Frank Wall Street Reform and Consumer Protection Act,* § 117. They can appeal to the FSOC for a reversal of that presumption. Thus, this group of entities has, for all intents and purposes, already been identified as too big to fail.

10. Dodd-Frank's so-called Collins amendment applies certain new capital requirements more broadly to insured depositories and their holding companies. *Dodd-Frank Wall Street Reform and Consumer Protection Act,* § 171. Likewise, new Basel III requirements will affect banks of all sizes. The banking regulators have issued proposed revisions to their capital rules. See Office of the Comptroller of the Currency, "Regulatory Capital—Basel III and the Standardized and Advanced Approaches: Description; Notices of Proposed Rulemaking" (OCC 2012-24, US Department of the Treasury, Washington, DC, August 30, 2012), http://www.occ.gov /news-issuances/bulletins/2012/bulletin-2012-24.html. The document provides links to the three joint agency proposals "to revise and replace the agencies' regulatory capital rules."

11. *Dodd-Frank Wall Street Reform and Consumer Protection Act,* §§ 161, 163, 165, and 166. In addition, Dodd-Frank grants the FSOC the authority to recommend specific enhanced regulations to the Federal Reserve. *Dodd-Frank Wall Street Reform and Consumer Protection Act,* § 115.

12. Home country regulators of foreign financial companies may resist regulatory efforts by the Fed, although Dodd-Frank directs the Fed to take foreign regulation

into account. *Dodd-Frank Wall Street Reform and Consumer Protection Act*, § 165(b)(2).

13. Under Dodd-Frank, systemically important entities have to devise so-called living wills (resolution plans). *Dodd-Frank Wall Street Reform and Consumer Protection Act,* § 165(d). The existence of such a plan does not change the Fed's incentive not to admit that it has allowed a firm to reach the point that it needs to use the plan.

14. See, for example, Peter Schroeder, "Dodd-Frank Panel Faces Pushback on Rules for Naming Vital Wall Street Firms," *The Hill: On the Money* (March 11, 2012), http://thehill.com/blogs/on-the-money/banking-financial-institutions/215373-dodd -frank-panel-faces-pushback-on-rules-for-naming-vital-wall-street-firms. The article discusses opposition to FSOC designations.

15. *Dodd-Frank Wall Street Reform and Consumer Protection Act,* § 113(h).

16. The president has nominated Richard Berner to be director of the OFR, but as of November 1, 2012, he had not been confirmed by the Senate.

17. The FSOC's expenses are treated as expenses of and paid for by the OFR. *Dodd-Frank Wall Street Reform and Consumer Protection Act,* § 118. In the OFR's budget discussions, the Treasury secretary, as chairman of the council, will presumably be concerned primarily about securing adequate funding for the FSOC rather than reining in the OFR.

18. For the first two years after the enactment of Dodd-Frank, the OFR was funded by the Fed. The Treasury estimated that 50 banks and bank holding companies would be assessed in the initial round. If the FSOC designates nonbank financial companies, they will also be assessed. Department of the Treasury, "Assessment of Fees on Large Bank Holding Companies and Nonbank Financial Companies Supervised by the Federal Reserve Board to Cover the Expenses of the Financial Research Fund," Notice of Final Rulemaking and Interim Final Rule, *Federal Register* 77 (May 21, 2012), 29884, note 14.

19. *Dodd-Frank Wall Street Reform and Consumer Protection Act,* § 154(b)(6).

What Title II does:

Title II establishes an FDIC-run resolution alternative
to bankruptcy, "Orderly Liquidation Authority."

Why Title II's approach is flawed:

Instead of reforming the bankruptcy model, Title II
abandons it in favor of a new, murky process.

Criteria for selecting companies for this nonbankruptcy option are
vague enough to make many companies potential resolution targets.

A decision to put a company through resolution is
subject to only limited judicial oversight.

Once a company is in resolution, the FDIC has broad discretion, without
effective checks, to determine how creditors' claims are handled.

TITLE II
Resolution

ITLE II OF Dodd-Frank creates an alternative to bankruptcy for certain financial companies. This title was an attempt to address an issue that arose during the financial crisis, namely the feasibility of having a major financial company go through the usual bankruptcy process. Drafters of Title II worried about bankruptcy courts' ability to handle complex financial companies and the domino effect a bankruptcy could have in the financial system. As manifested in Dodd-Frank, however, the resolution alternative gives tremendous authority to the government to shut companies down with almost no oversight.

As an initial matter, it is worth noting that concerns about the ability of the normal bankruptcy process to handle large financial entities may be overstated. Bankruptcy courts routinely handle complex bankruptcies. Lehman's bankruptcy—although certainly messy, as most large bankruptcies are—does not support a conclusion that bankruptcy is unworkable. David Skeel's excellent analysis of the "Lehman Myth" is helpful in this regard. Skeel concludes: "Given the tumultuous environment in which Lehman filed its original bankruptcy petition, the assumption that bankruptcy must have been a disaster is perhaps understandable. But, in fact, bankruptcy worked quite well."[1] Rather than creating a process distinct from bankruptcy, Congress could have looked at ways to modify the existing bankruptcy process so it would function more smoothly and quickly for large financial companies.[2]

Under the Orderly Liquidation Authority, as the Title II resolution is called, financial companies in default or in danger of default are resolved through an alternative process to bankruptcy. Different rules apply than would apply in bankruptcy, and the FDIC, instead of a bankruptcy court, runs the process.[3] The FDIC, in its role, has broad discretion to determine how creditors' claims will be handled. Creditors are entitled to receive at least what they would if the company had been liquidated under Chapter 7 of the Bankruptcy Code,[4] but this may not be a meaningful floor.[5] The FDIC has the power to treat similarly situated creditors differently. Another distinguishing feature from bankruptcy is that the FDIC can move some or all of the risk of bad assets to the taxpayer, thus making the company a more attractive target for an acquirer.[6] The FDIC has suggested that it might choose to rejuvenate a failing company with the help of government debt guarantees instead of winding it down and selling its solvent parts.[7]

Because the FDIC has broad powers under Title II, the process—or lack thereof—for selecting the companies that will go through orderly liquidation is particularly troubling. Congress sacrificed transparency and perhaps even constitutionality at the feet of speed and flexibility for government regulators. As a result, the government can seize and dissolve companies with almost no opportunity for the company or its creditors to object. Because "all financial companies" are potentially eligible for resolution under Title II, resolution may be used on companies that have not previously been designated by the FSOC as systemically important.

The Treasury secretary, upon receipt of a recommendation from other financial regulators and in consultation with the president, must proceed to put a company into orderly liquidation if seven open-ended criteria are met.[8] The first criterion, that the company must be in default or in danger of default, could, during a time of severe distress in the economy, apply to almost any company. Second, the failure of the company, in the absence of a Title II resolution, "would have serious adverse effects on financial stability in the United States." During a financial crisis, it is easy to anticipate there will be serious adverse effects from the failure of any large financial firm. Third, the Treasury secretary has to determine there is no private-sector alternative for *preventing* the company's default. Thus, even a private-sector post-default alternative would not suffice. Fourth, the secretary has to conclude that any effects on shareholders, creditors, and counterparties are appropriate when balanced against the benefits of a Title II resolution. Fifth, the secretary has to consider resolution's ability to mitigate the adverse effects of failure. The sixth criterion is the only definitive one: a federal regulator must have ordered that all of the company's convertible debt be converted. The final criterion, that the company must be a "financial company," makes a wide range of companies potentially subject to seizure.[9]

Once the Treasury secretary has identified a company for resolution, it will notify the company. If the company fails to acquiesce to FDIC receivership,[10] the secretary will file a sealed petition with the federal district court. The court then has 24 hours to consider the petition to liquidate the company.[11] Accordingly, the company has less than one day to make its case that it should not be liquidated. The whole process is, under the threat of criminal penalties—including up to five years in prison—confidential and nonpublic. The nonpublic nature of the proceedings makes it difficult for a company to demonstrate that the Treasury secretary has erred in selecting it for liquidation, because the company will have difficulty soliciting outside assistance. Presumably, creditors and shareholders, who would have a great interest in the court's ruling, would not be permitted to know of the secretary's petition.

In assessing the Treasury's determination to liquidate the company, the court may consider only two of the criteria underlying the determination.[12] Specifically, the statute directs the court to consider the Treasury secretary's determinations that the company is a financial company and that it is in default or in danger of default. If the court finds either of these determinations "arbitrary and capricious," which is a legal standard tilted in favor of the government, the court has to "immediately" provide the Treasury with an explanation of its determination so the Treasury can refile its petition in a manner that addresses the court's concerns. If the district court rules in the Treasury's favor, appeals to the Court of Appeals and subsequently the Supreme Court are permitted.[13] However, the liquidation will proceed despite the appeal, and consideration by the Court of Appeals and Supreme Court is of the same limited scope as the district court's consideration. No room is allowed for a challenge of the constitutionality of the Treasury secretary's action.

That the Treasury secretary, with limited judicial oversight, can seize a solvent company and hand it over to the FDIC to be wound down outside of the normal bankruptcy process is a startling challenge to basic property rights.[14] The new grants of power to regulators under Title II may encourage companies to spend more of their resources currying favor with government officials.[15] While the reasonableness of the Treasury secretary and other government officials involved in making the decision may be a source of restraint on the use of this power, historically, American government has relied not on the reasonableness of the people in office but on effective institutional checks and balances on their power.[16] Such checks are particularly important during crises, when the temptation to act is great. Title II represents a troubling opportunity for the government to intervene dramatically in the private marketplace without meaningful restraint.[17]

Title II

NOTES

1. David A. Skeel, *The New Financial Deal: Understanding the Dodd-Frank Act and Its (Unintended) Consequences* (Hoboken, NJ: John Wiley and Sons, 2011), 31. See also Thomas J. Fitzpatrick IV and James B. Thomson, "How Well Does Bankruptcy Work When Large Financial Firms Fail? Some Lessons from Lehman Brothers," *Economic Commentary* (Federal Reserve Bank of Cleveland), October 26, 2011, http://www.clevelandfed.org/research/commentary/2011/2011-23.cfm. Fitzpatrick and Thomson argue that although the Lehman bankruptcy is hard to analyze given the environment during which it occurred, "based on the experience with Lehman, there is no clear evidence that bankruptcy law is insufficient to handle the resolution of large, complex financial firms." Although not looking specifically at bankruptcy process issues, Jean Helwege and Gaiyan Zhang find that "Both creditors and competitors of bankrupt firms experience negative valuation effects around Chapter 11 filings and the effects are larger for firms with greater exposures in cases of counterparty contagion and for firms with more closely related businesses in cases of information contagion. However, the magnitude of the effects is modest in either case and would not likely bring down a financial system." The authors found "stronger counterparty contagion effects for Lehman Brothers and AIG but even these extreme events did not involve sufficient counterparty contagion to cause numerous cascading bankruptcies in the financial system." See Jean Helwege and Gaiyan Zhang, "Financial Firm Bankruptcy and Contagion" (working paper, University of South Carolina and University of Missouri–St. Louis, Columbia, SC, and St. Louis, MO, July 31, 2012), 2 and 35, http://papers.ssrn.com/sol3/papers.cfm?abstract_id=2136246.

2. For a description of potential modifications to make bankruptcy function better for large, complex financial institutions, see generally Fed, "Study on the Resolution of Financial Companies under the Bankruptcy Code," Report to Congress, July 2011, notes 78–80 and accompanying text, http://www.federalreserve.gov/publications/other-reports/bankruptcy-financial-study-201107.htm#f3r. Serious thought has been given to how a financial-firm specific bankruptcy regime would look. See Thomas H. Jackson, "Bankruptcy Code Chapter 14: A Proposal" (working paper, Hoover Institution Resolution Project, Stanford, CA, February 28, 2012), http://media.hoover.org/sites/default/files/documents/Bankruptcy-Code-Chapter-14-Proposal-20120228.pdf; and Thomas H. Jackson, Kenneth E. Scott, Kimberly Anne Summe, and John B. Taylor, "Resolution of Failed Financial Institutions: Orderly Liquidation Authority and a New Chapter 14" (study, Hoover Institution Resolution Project, Stanford, CA, April 25, 2011), http://media.hoover.org/sites/default/files/documents/Resolution-Project-Booklet.pdf. The FDIC recently has

expressed "support [for] improvements to the Bankruptcy Code that would better allow for the failure of a large complex financial institution without broad systemic disruption." See Stephanie Gleason, "Academics Want to Give Chapter 14 a Chance," *Wall Street Journal: SmartMoney*, September 19, 2012. Another option would be to create a speed-bankruptcy mechanism such that if the company ran into trouble, long-term debt could be converted to equity. Garett Jones with Ben Klutsey and Katelyn Christ, "Speed Bankruptcy: A Firewall to Future Crises" (working paper 10-02, Mercatus Center at George Mason University, Arlington, VA, January 2010), http://mercatus.org/sites/default/files/publication/WP1002_Speed%20Bankruptcy%20-%20A%20Firewall%20to%20Future%20Crises.pdf. Jones, Klutsey, and Christ recommend fast-track debt-to-equity conversions as an alternative to government recapitalization of institutions.

3. See, for example, Hollace T. Cohen, "Orderly Liquidation Authority: A New Insolvency Regime to Address Systemic Risk," *University of Richmond Law Review* 45, no. 4 (2011): 1227–28. Cohen writes, "The purpose of the Bankruptcy Code is to maximize recoveries to creditors and other stakeholders, while a primary purpose of Title II is to avoid a disorderly liquidation that could have an adverse effect on the financial stability of the United States. As a result of these different goals, Title II will likely have a profound effect on the rights of creditors, other stakeholders, and the debtor itself as they exist under the Bankruptcy Code."

4. *Dodd-Frank Wall Street Reform and Consumer Protection Act,* § 210(d)(2).

5. See Douglas G. Baird and Edward R. Morrison, "Dodd-Frank for Bankruptcy Lawyers," *American Bankruptcy Institute Law Review* 19, no. 2 (Winter 2011): 287, 316. The authors write, "To determine the minimum recovery to creditors, we must imagine the liquidation value of the institution in an economy that is suffering an economic collapse. That liquidation value is likely to be close to zero."

6. The FDIC modeled what a Lehman failure would have looked like post-Dodd-Frank. The FDIC's successful resolution of Lehman turned on the assumption that Barclay's would have purchased Lehman because the FDIC would have been able to "alleviate Barclays' concerns" by sharing in the losses associated with the problem assets. More generally, the FDIC noted that

> Loss-share transactions allow the FDIC to obtain better bids from potential assuming institutions by sharing a portion of the risk on a pool of assets. This has been particularly important during periods of uncertainty about the value of assets. The FDIC's experience has been that these transactions result in both better bid prices and improved recoveries for the receivership and receivership creditors.

FDIC, "The Orderly Liquidation of Lehman Brothers Holdings Inc. under the

Dodd-Frank Act," *FDIC Quarterly* 5, no. 2 (May 2011): 16 and note 68, http://www .fdic.gov/bank/analytical/quarterly/2011_vol5_2/lehman.pdf. If the availability of the government to step in and assume losses related to bad assets is the reason the Title II resolution will work better than bankruptcy, it is not clear that the Title II resolution is distinguishable from the 2008 bailouts. The government also can fund resolutions directly, but taxpayers are supposed to be repaid over a number of years through assessments on financial companies. *Dodd-Frank Wall Street Reform and Consumer Protection Act,* §§ 210(n), 210(o), and 214.

7. See Martin J. Gruenberg, acting chairman, FDIC, "Remarks to the Federal Reserve Bank of Chicago Bank Structure Conference" (speech, Federal Reserve Bank of Chicago Bank Structure Conference, Chicago, IL, May 10, 2012), http://www .fdic.gov/news/news/speeches/chairman/spmay1012.html. Gruenberg explains the FDIC's resolution strategy, which would include "converting the failed firm through the public receivership process into a new, well-capitalized and viable private sector entity." See also Morrison Foerster, "Orderly Liquidation Authority: FDIC Announces Its Strategy," news release, May 16, 2012, 5–6, http://www .mofo.com/files/Uploads/Images/120516-Orderly-Liquidation-Authority-FDIC-An nounces-Its-Strategy.pdf. The release observes, "Under the OLA [orderly liquidation authority], a bridge company is not really a 'bridge' to anything. Rather, the company is a refinanced and nominally recapitalized version of the failed institution, with some of the same stakeholders, albeit with different stakes. By contrast, the FDIC has used the bridge company in bank receiverships to facilitate the sale of good assets to a new buyer and the liquidation of bad assets."

8. *Dodd-Frank Wall Street Reform and Consumer Protection Act,* § 203(b). The Fed and the FDIC, at the request of the Treasury secretary or on their own initiative, can vote to make a written recommendation that a company should be liquidated under Title II. In certain cases, the Securities and Exchange Commission (SEC) or the director of the Federal Insurance Office is involved in making the recommendation.

9. Financial companies include any bank holding company, nonbank financial company designated under Title I for special regulation by the Fed, any company that is "predominantly [that is, 85 percent or more of revenue] engaged in activities that the [Fed] has determined are financial or incidental thereto for purposes of section 4(k) of the Bank Holding Company Act of 1956 [U.S. Code 12 (1956), §§ 1843(k)]," or any financial subsidiary of any of those companies. *Dodd-Frank Wall Street Reform and Consumer Protection Act,* § 201(a)(11). The FDIC has undertaken to define "financial in nature" for purposes of Title II. See FDIC, "Definition of 'Predominantly Engaged in Activities That Are Financial in Nature or Incidental Thereto,'" Notice of Proposed Rulemaking, *Federal Register* 77 (June 18, 2012), 36194. In doing so, it has proposed to follow the Fed's interpretation of that term

for purposes of Title I. See Fed, "Definition of 'Predominantly Engaged in Financial Activities,'" Supplemental Notice of Proposed Rulemaking and Request for Comment, *Federal Register* 77 (April 10, 2012), 21494, 21496. The Fed proposed to remove the "non-definitional conditions" used to describe permissible activities for financial holding companies under section 4(k) of the Bank Holding Company Act, which has the effect of broadening the companies potentially covered by Titles I and II. See ibid. Both agencies have been criticized for interpreting the term more broadly than warranted by Dodd-Frank. Senators David Vitter and Mark Pryor object that the Fed's proposal would result in commercial enterprises being captured under Title I. See letter from David Vitter and Mark Pryor, US Senators, to Ben Bernanke, chairman, Fed, May 16, 2012, http://www.federalreserve.gov /SECRS/2012/June/20120626/R-1405/R-1405_062512_107849_444554712632_1 .pdf. The US Chamber of Commerce argues that "the actual legislative history, Congressional intent, and the overall structure of the Act do not support—much less favor—the Board's expansive interpretation of its authority to dissociate financial activities for nonbanks from the specific activities regulated financial institutions may engage in consistent with section 4(k)." See letter from David T. Hirschmann, president and CEO, US Chamber of Commerce Center for Capital Markets Competitiveness, to Jennifer J. Johnson, secretary, Fed, May 25, 2012, 10, http://www.fdic.gov/regulations/laws/federal/2012/2012-ad73-c_02.PDF. The Chamber also "believes that the Board improperly altered a Congressional directive defining activities that are financial in nature under Title I. By logical extension, the FDIC should not use the Board's flawed NPRM as the foundational standard upon which the Supplemental Notice is built." Letter from Tom Quaadman, vice president, US Chamber of Commerce Center for Capital Markets Competitiveness, to Robert E. Feldman, executive secretary, FDIC, August 6, 2012, 2, http://www.fdic.gov/regulations/laws/federal/2012/2012-ad73-c_02supp.pdf.

10. Boards would feel considerable pressure to assent, particularly because *Dodd-Frank Wall Street Reform and Consumer Protection Act*, § 207, removes their legal liability for doing so. See Baird and Morrison, "Dodd-Frank for Bankruptcy Lawyers," 294. They write, "Board members will likely see the folly of trying to fight off the Secretary, the Federal Reserve, and the FDIC simultaneously. Moreover, they will also look to the comfort provided by § 207, which protects them from liability for consenting in good faith to the receivership."

11. If the court fails to meet the deadline, the company is immediately put into FDIC receivership. In rules issued by the US District Court for the District of Columbia with respect to Title II, the court directs the Treasury secretary to provide written notice that a petition would be filed at least 48 hours in advance of filing, "to the extent feasible." US District Court for the District of Columbia, Amendment to Local Civil Rule 85, *Filings under the Dodd-Frank Wall Street Reform and Consumer*

Protection Act (Washington, DC: US District Court, July 6, 2011), http://www.dcd .uscourts.gov/dcd/sites/dcd/files/2011_LCvR_85_Dodd-Frank_Amended.pdf.

12. *Dodd-Frank Wall Street Reform and Consumer Protection Act*, § 202(a)(1)(A)(iv).

13. Ibid., § 202(a)(2).

14. See, for example, C. Boyden Gray and John Shu, "The Dodd-Frank Wall Street Reform and Consumer Protection Act of 2010: Is It Constitutional?," *Engage* (December 2010). Gray and Shu identify constitutional deficiencies in, among other places, Title II of Dodd-Frank and observe that Title II "essentially overrides the bankruptcy code and its judicial review options, thus inappropriately authorizing agency bureaucrats and political appointees instead of the impartial judiciary to determine basic contract rights."

15. For this point, the author credits an anonymous reviewer.

16. For a discussion of constitutional flaws with Title II's resolution regime, see Brent J. Horton, "How Dodd–Frank's Orderly Liquidation Authority for Financial Companies Violates Article III of the United States Constitution," *Journal of Corporate Law* 36 (2011): 869, 873. Horton argues that "all that Dodd–Frank accomplishes is substituting one flawed system for another, while trampling the Constitution."

17. As one example of the potential lack of restraint, the FDIC has suggested, on the grounds that otherwise the arrival of the FDIC would signal that a firm was troubled, a continuous FDIC presence at firms eligible for resolution. The FDIC explains, "While it is possible in this situation or in other situations that the FDIC's on site presence could create signaling concerns, this argues for the FDIC having a continuous on-site presence for resolution planning during good times." See FDIC, "The Orderly Liquidation of Lehman Brothers Holdings Inc. under the Dodd-Frank Act," 11.

What Title III does:

Title III eliminates the Office of Thrift Supervision and assigns its responsibilities to the Office of the Comptroller of the Currency and the Fed.

It raises federal deposit insurance to $250,000.

It expands the assessment base for deposit insurance to total consolidated assets minus tangible equity.

It creates an Office of Minority and Women Inclusion at financial regulatory agencies.

Why Title III's approach is flawed:

Expansion of deposit insurance decreases effective market restraint of bank risk taking and may yield greater systemic instability.

Title III adds a new layer of bureaucracy at each financial regulator.

TITLE III
Ending the Office of Thrift Supervision

T ITLE III OF Dodd-Frank is primarily designed to transfer the functions previously performed by the Office of Thrift Supervision (OTS) to other bank regulators. Its oversight of thrifts passed to the Office of the Comptroller of the Currency (OCC), and its responsibility for thrift holding companies was moved to the Fed.[1] The change is a reflection of the negative assessment of the quality of OTS's supervision of entities like Countrywide, IndyMac, and AIG.

Confused lines of regulatory responsibility were a contributor to the crisis, so eliminating one federal financial regulator was a positive step toward regulatory simplification, which facilitates regulatory accountability.[2] Unfortunately, in the aggregate, Dodd-Frank failed meaningfully to consolidate the regulatory apparatus and even added another front-line federal financial regulator, the Consumer Financial Protection Bureau (CFPB).[3]

Title III did more than eliminate the OTS, however. Hidden in the middle of the title are a number of changes to deposit insurance. Deposit insurance began in 1934 with $2,500 per depositor in coverage. The limit was increased to $5,000 later that year, $10,000 in 1950, and was bumped from $40,000 to $100,000 in 1980. It stayed there until a temporary increase during the crisis raised the limit to $250,000. Dodd-Frank made the $250,000-per-depositor limit permanent.[4] In addition, Title III extended unlimited deposit insurance on noninterest-bearing transaction accounts, such as checking accounts, until the end of 2012.[5]

Although deposit insurance has taken deep root in the American banking system as an effective way to prevent runs by bank depositors, it distorts incentives in the banking system and may not, on balance, help consumers.[6] President Franklin D. Roosevelt, his Treasury secretary, and many others at the time of its introduction opposed federal deposit insurance.[7] One of the reasons underlying opposition to deposit insurance was a fear that it would dull banks' risk management. Deposit insurance decreases depositors' incentive to monitor banks because they know that the government will make good on the bank's promises if the bank fails to do so. The consequence may be greater systemic instability.[8] Deposit insurance may also encourage overconcentration of household assets in bank accounts.[9] Finally, the administration of deposit insurance is not free.[10]

One important way to limit the harmful effects of deposit insurance is to cap the amount the insurance will cover.[11] Dodd-Frank did the opposite: it dramatically increased coverage. Even though an argument can be made that small depositors who cannot monitor banks effectively should be federally insured,[12] extending insurance to depositors with $250,000 protects a group of people who do not need that protection. Even with a lower limit, these depositors could spread their deposits across multiple banks and remain fully protected. Dodd-Frank, which is supposed to address moral-hazard concerns, took a step to increase moral hazard in the financial system. Moreover, Dodd-Frank extended deposit insurance at a time when the Deposit Insurance Fund (DIF) was already under great stress.[13]

Title III also expands the assessment base for deposit insurance; now it is based on total consolidated assets minus tangible equity rather than insured deposits.[14] This change effectively shifts more of the assessment burden from community banks onto bigger banks. This shift could embolden these larger institutions to demand a government bailout in the future based on the fact that they have borne a disproportionate amount of the DIF assessment burden. Dodd-Frank also mandated a long-term target minimum reserve ratio for the crisis-depleted DIF of 1.35 percent.[15]

Title III mandates that most of the federal financial regulators create an Office of Minority and Women Inclusion.[16] The goal of increasing diversity at financial regulators is commendable, but these new offices will have an outsized ability to affect the agencies' regulated entities. The director of each office is charged with developing standards for "assessing the diversity policies and procedures of entities regulated by the agency." The regulators, whose pools of regulated entities overlap, are reportedly working together to develop a common approach to assessing the entities they regulate.[17] Given the large numbers of entities regulated by these agencies, the inclusion offices could affect hiring practices throughout the financial industry. It is important that diversity goals be achieved in a manner consistent with other regulatory objectives, including safety and soundness.

In sum, Title III, by eliminating one regulator in an overly broad field of federal financial regulators, takes a step in the right direction. Nevertheless, by increasing deposit insurance, Title III has further entrenched the government, instead of the market, as the primary monitor of banks.

NOTES

1. Dodd-Frank consolidated the Fed's authority as holding-company regulator.
2. Regulatory consolidation facilitates regulatory accountability because if the regulator for a particular firm or activity is clearly identified, it is harder for it to escape responsibility. Regulatory consolidation also lowers costs for regulated entities, which are not forced to contend with multiple, and sometimes conflicting,

regulators' views of the world. On the other hand, regulatory consolidation can facilitate regulatory capture and make it harder for regulatory mistakes to be kept in check. For an insightful discussion of why the existence of multiple bank regulators is not necessarily bad and why, in fact, the regulatory competition might be good, see Mark Calabria, "Would Consolidating Regulators Avoid the Next Crisis?" *Lombard Street* 1, no. 16 (November 16, 2009), http://www.cato.org/pubs/articles /calabria-would-consolidating-regulators-avoid-next-crisis.pdf.

3. The CFPB, unlike other bank regulators, does not have safety and soundness responsibilities but, as will be discussed in the section on Title X, has a narrow consumer protection focus. Splitting up safety and soundness and consumer protection considerations could adversely affect the stability of financial institutions.

4. *Dodd-Frank Wall Street Reform and Consumer Protection Act*, § 335. The $250,000 cap was made effective back to January 1, 2008, so it would cover depositors in banks that failed during the crisis.

5. Ibid., § 343.

6. Deposit insurance is a relatively new addition to the federal banking framework in the United States and throughout the world. Macey and Miller offer a public-choice analysis of why deposit insurance is so common, despite the fact that it is not a net benefit to consumers:

> Applying the public choice theory of regulation to the issue of deposit insurance, the logic of protecting depositors is clear. The primary beneficiaries of this sort of protection are the banks themselves: government guarantees of their liabilities enhance their credit and therefore lower their costs of doing business. Government guarantees of bank liabilities are less helpful to depositors than they appear, since some, if not all, of the benefits of credit enhancement are eroded by the lower interest rates banks must pay for deposits. The distinct political advantage of government guarantees of bank liabilities is that such guarantees rarely, if ever, meet with concerted political opposition. This is because the diffuse citizens who must bear the costs of these programs generally view themselves as beneficiaries of the schemes, which are marketed by bureaucrats, politicians and interest groups as consumer protection devices.

Jonathan R. Macey and Geoffrey P. Miller, "Deposit Insurance, The Implicit Regulatory Contract, and the Mismatch in the Term Structure of Banks' Assets and Liabilities," *Yale Journal on Regulation* 12, no. 1 (1995): 19. See also Eugene N. White, "The Legacy of Deposit Insurance: The Growth, Spread, and Cost of Insuring Financial Intermediaries," in *The Defining Moment: The Great Depression and the*

American Economy in the Twentieth Century, ed. Michael D. Bordo, Claudia Goldin, and Eugene N. White (Chicago: University of Chicago Press, 1998), 90, http://www .nber.org/chapters/c6889.pdf. White explains, "Far from being a high-minded policy aimed at protecting the depositor, the design of the Federal Deposit Insurance Corporation (FDIC) was the product of a lengthy legislative struggle, pitting smaller state-chartered, often unit banks against larger banks, often members of the Federal Reserve System."

7. FDIC, "A Brief History of Deposit Insurance in the United States" (paper prepared for International Conference on Deposit Insurance, Washington, DC, September 1998), 25, http://www.fdic.gov/bank/historical/brief/brhist.pdf.

8. See, for example, Asli Demirgü-Kunt and Enrica Detragiache, "Does Deposit Insurance Increase Banking System Stability? An Empirical Investigation," *Journal of Monetary Economics* 49 (2002): 1378, 1402. The authors write, "According to economic theory, while deposit insurance may increase bank stability by reducing self-fulfilling or information-driven depositor runs, it may decrease bank stability by encouraging risk taking on the part of banks." Demirgü-Kunt and Detragiache found, based on a 61-country study, that "explicit deposit insurance tends to be detrimental to bank stability," although good regulatory systems can partially offset the harm. The international experience with deposit insurance is illuminating, although many other countries adopted deposit insurance only in the last 20 years. See, for example, Lucy Chernykh and Rebel A. Cole, "Does Deposit Insurance Improve Financial Intermediation? Evidence from the Russian Experiment," *Journal of Banking and Finance* 35 (2011): 400. Chernykh and Cole conclude that there is "both a dark side and a bright side of deposit insurance," which, when introduced in Russia, increased retail deposits but also resulted in banks' taking greater risks.

9. For this point, the author credits an anonymous reviewer.

10. See Thomas L. Hogan and William J. Luther, "Explicit and Implicit Costs of Government-Provided Deposit Insurance" (working paper, West Texas A&M University and Kenyon College, Canyon, TX, and Gambier, OH, June 13, 2012), 11, http:// papers.ssrn.com/sol3/papers.cfm?abstract_id=2083662.

11. See, for example, Patricia A. McCoy, "The Moral Hazard Implications of Deposit Insurance: Theory and Evidence" (paper presented at Seminar on Current Developments in Monetary and Financial Law, Washington, DC, October 23–27, 2006, draft dated February 18, 2007), 16, http://www.imf.org/external/np/seminars/eng/2006 /mfl/pam.pdf. McCoy explains, "The research on coverage limits strongly counsels governments to place credible coverage limits on deposit insurance guarantees in order to put large creditors of banks on notice that their deposits are not safe."

12. Small depositors are unlikely to monitor banks directly, which is why many jurisdictions have chosen to cover them with deposit insurance. Nevertheless, because larger depositors can monitor banks or hire someone to do so, an argument could

be made for paring back deposit insurance. Higher levels of deposit insurance do appear correlated to the risk of instability in the banking system. Demirgü-Kunt and Detragiache, "Does Deposit Insurance Increase Banking System Stability? An Empirical Investigation," *Journal of Monetary Economics* 49 (2002): 1386.

13. At the end of 2010, the DIF balance was negative $7.4 billion, up from a low of negative $20.9 billion in 2009. FDIC, *2011 Annual Report* (Washington, DC: FDIC, April 30, 2012), 130, http://www.fdic.gov/about/strategic/report/2011annualreport/AR 11final.pdf.

14. *Dodd-Frank Wall Street Reform and Consumer Protection Act,* § 331(b).

15. Ibid., § 334. As of December 31, 2011, the ratio of reserves to estimated insured deposits was only 0.17 percent.

16. Ibid., § 342. The director is charged with developing diversity standards for the agency and its contractors and has the authority to recommend the termination of any contractor that "has failed to make a good faith effort to include minorities and women in their workforce." The agency head must act in response to that recommendation. Ibid., § 342(c)(3). Depending on how the standards develop, this provision could have major effects on how contracts are awarded by financial regulators. See Andrew R. Mavraganis and Cristina L. Meng, "Dodd-Frank Section 342: Office of Minority and Women Inclusion," Pepper Hamilton LLP, July 16, 2012, http://www.lexology.com/library/detail.aspx?g=ce340ae9-e0e2-43d1-9a19 -c05e2402b35d. Current contracting practices by federal financial regulators are not particularly transparent, an issue that is discussed further in the section on Title XI.

17. See, for example, Fed Board of Governors, *Report to the Congress on the Office of Minority and Women Inclusion,* 112th Cong., 2d sess. (March 2012), 13, http://www .federalreserve.gov/publications/other-reports/files/omwi-report-20120402.pdf.

What Title IV does:

Title IV requires advisers to hedge funds and other private funds to register with the Securities and Exchange Commission (SEC).

It raises the threshold for adviser registration with the SEC, which moves more advisers to state regulation.

It prevents investors from counting their residence toward the net-wealth threshold to qualify for investing in hedge funds.

Why Title IV's approach is flawed:

SEC resources will be diverted from monitoring advisers who manage the assets of average retail investors to monitoring the assets of wealthy investors who invest in private funds.

Regulators have devised an unnecessarily costly compliance regime for private funds, the costs of which will be passed on to investors.

TITLE IV
Hedge Funds

A LTHOUGH HEDGE FUNDS and other private funds were not central to the financial crisis, Title IV of Dodd-Frank makes sweeping changes to the way they are regulated. A 2004 attempt by the Securities and Exchange Commission (SEC) to require advisers to hedge funds to register with the SEC was struck down in court.[1] Proponents of hedge-fund-adviser registration took advantage of Dodd-Frank as an opportunity to overturn the court ruling and give this authority to the SEC. Under Title IV of Dodd-Frank, advisers to hedge funds and private-equity funds are required to register with the SEC, and the SEC is required to conduct periodic inspections.[2]

One consequence of the new private-fund-adviser registration requirement is that SEC resources will be diverted from monitoring advisers who manage the assets of average retail investors to monitoring the assets of those wealthy enough to invest in private funds. In fact, because of another Title IV change, fewer people will be eligible to invest in hedge funds and other limited investment opportunities. Under Section 413 of the act, an individual will no longer be able to count the value of her primary residence toward the $1 million net-worth minimum threshold for accredited investor status.[3] Accredited investor status opens the door to opportunities to invest in securities unavailable to other investors.[4]

Although likely motivated by a desire to protect people from making investments inappropriate for them, the effect of the change is to further limit the investment options of people who are not wealthy. When hedge-fund advisers were not required to register with the SEC, one could argue—although not without a paternalistic bent—that the SEC needed to prevent investors who could not afford to lose money from investing in those funds. The new registration and examination regime for hedge-fund advisers makes this argument more difficult. It raises questions about why the government is allocating its limited resources in a way that benefits the small number of Americans whom the government permits to invest in hedge funds.[5]

Even though Dodd-Frank provided an exemption from registration for venture-capital-fund advisers, that exemption may prove illusory under the weight of SEC rules. Venture capital funds are still subject to recordkeeping and reporting requirements. SEC commissioner Troy A. Paredes explains the problems associated with the SEC's treatment of venture-capital-fund advisers:

> The extent of the mandatory public disclosure that the final rule imposes on [venture-capital] fund managers, even though they are exempt from registration, coupled with the rationales that animate the release in requiring such disclosure, goes too far toward collapsing the distinction between what it means to be unregistered versus registered as an investment adviser. I am troubled that the release charts an increasingly regulatory course forward such that the Advisers Act regime that applies to exempt advisers will end up closely resembling the regime that regulates registered advisers; that as their reporting and recordkeeping obligations mount, exempt advisers will find themselves subject to what in substance is registration.[6]

Paredes also points out that a drafting nuance in Dodd-Frank exposes venture-capital-fund advisers to examination by the SEC, even though they are exempt from registration.[7]

While Dodd-Frank's new regulatory regime for private-fund advisers appears to have been motivated largely by investor-protection concerns, Title IV also reflects systemic-risk concerns, namely concerns that hedge funds are contributing to the instability of the financial system and therefore need to be tracked more closely. These concerns are not backed by evidence that hedge funds contributed to the occurrence or severity of the financial crisis. Sections 404 and 406 of Dodd-Frank require the collection of a broad range of information from advisers to private funds "as necessary and appropriate in the public interest and for the protection of investors, or for the assessment of systemic risk by the Financial Stability Oversight Council." The FSOC may use this information to designate private funds or their advisers as nonbank financial entities in need of special regulation by the Fed, a designation likely to be interpreted by the markets as a too-big-to-fail indicator.

Dodd-Frank's broad and ambiguous information-collection goals were interpreted by the SEC and the CFTC in the new Form PF.[8] Form PF requires all but the smallest advisers to hedge funds (including commodity pools), private equity funds, and liquidity funds to provide detailed information about fund investors, investment strategies, counterparties, financing, and portfolio composition and characteristics. Given its lengthy, complicated, and often unclear information demands, Form PF imposes a substantial burden on the advisers to which it applies.[9] As with other regulatory costs, the costs of these new rules will be passed on to investors.

As has been typical of many Dodd-Frank rules, the superficial economic analysis associated with Form PF failed to consider the full costs of the new form.[10] With respect to benefits, the regulators "anticipate . . . that Form PF will improve the information available to regulators as they seek to prevent or mitigate the effects of future financial crises, and if this information helps to avoid even a small portion of the costs of a financial crisis like the most recent one, the benefits of Form PF will be very significant."[11] The failure to look more precisely at the need for the information being requested and the direct and indirect costs of producing it, including potentially compromising proprietary information, may cause Form PF to harm investors without assisting regulators in identifying future problems.

Title IV creates a new, intensive regulatory regime for advisers to private funds. In doing so, Dodd-Frank threatens to drive funds off-shore, harm investors, and make it more likely, not less, that these funds will one day be the recipients of government largesse. This is an unfortunate development, because hedge funds and other private funds have generally emerged and disappeared in response to market forces, not government intervention.

NOTES

1. *Goldstein v. SEC*, 451 F.3d 873, 877 (D.C. Cir. 2006).
2. But see *Dodd-Frank Wall Street Reform and Consumer Protection Act*, § 407, which exempts certain venture capital advisers from registration; and *Dodd-Frank Wall Street Reform and Consumer Protection Act*, § 408, which provides for an exemption for advisers to private funds with less than $150 million under management.
3. Using 2007 data, the SEC staff estimated that only 7.2 percent of US households would have qualified as accredited investors under the net-worth test, the income test (which is an alternative test), or both. SEC, "Net Worth Standard for Accredited Investors," Notice of Final Rulemaking, *Federal Register* 76 (December 29, 2011), 81793, note 72.
4. Title IV may deny even wealthy Americans additional investment opportunities. By altering the private adviser exemption from registration, Section 403 makes it more likely that advisers to offshore funds that accept American investors will be forced to register with the SEC or be subject to reporting and recordkeeping requirements. As a consequence, some foreign advisers may go to great lengths to

avoid US investors. For an analysis of the changes and the potential implications for foreign advisers and US investors, see Kay A. Gordon and Joshua O'Melia, "Regulation of Offshore Advisers Expanded," *The Investment Lawyer* 19, no. 4 (April 2012): 4, http://www.bingham.com/Publications/Files/2012/04/Regulation-and-Supervision-of-Financial-Planning.

5. See, for example, Daniel Gallagher, commissioner, SEC, "Keynote Address" (speech, Investment Adviser Association Investment Adviser Compliance Conference, Arlington, VA, March 8, 2012), http://www.sec.gov/news/speech/2012/spch 030812dmg.htm. Gallagher explains that "this expansion of our regulatory reach will not serve to protect ordinary retail investors, but rather investors who could, as the Supreme Court so notably said, 'fend for themselves.'"

6. Troy Paredes, "Statement at Open Meeting to Adopt Final Rules Regarding Exemptions for Advisers to Venture Capital Funds, Private Fund Advisers with Less Than $150 Million in Assets under Management, and Foreign Private Advisers and Final Rules Implementing Amendments to the Investment Advisers Act of 1940" (speech, Washington, DC, June 22, 2011), http://www.sec.gov/news/speech/2011 /spch062211tap-items-1-2.htm#_ftnref1.

7. Ibid.

8. The new Form PF is primarily intended to provide information to the FSOC, but the CFTC and SEC will also use the information for their own regulatory and enforcement purposes. Form PF, which is filed with the SEC, is intended to be available to regulators, but not the public.

9. Form PF, including instructions and definitions, is 63 pages. Advisers may find that merely working through the requirements for determining which aspects of Form PF apply is likely to be quite time-consuming. The greater the assets an adviser has under management, the greater the amount and frequency of its reporting obligations. The largest advisers began filing at the end of August 2012. Smaller advisers were given more time to comply. See "Form PF: Reporting Form for Investment Advisers to Private Funds and Certain Commodity Pool Operators and Commodity Trading Advisers," OMB Number 3235-0679, expires December 31, 2014, http:// www.sec.gov/about/forms/formpf.pdf.

10. For example, the $108 million first-year costs and $60 million ongoing costs assume that risk and compliance personnel will bear responsibility for the form. SEC and CFTC, "Reporting by Investment Advisers to Private Funds and Certain Commodity Pool Operators and Commodity Trading Advisors on Form PF," Notice of Final Rulemaking, Federal Register 76 (November 16, 2011), 71128, 71168–69. Given the form's complexity and the fact that the form may be used as a basis for enforcement action against an adviser, pricey outside counsel is likely to be involved in the preparation of the form.

11. Ibid., 71166, 71171. The CFTC incongruously discussed purported benefits of the

rule in its analysis of the costs: "With respect to costs, the CFTC has determined that . . . without the reporting requirements imposed by this rulemaking, FSOC will not have sufficient information to identify and address potential threats to the financial stability of the United States (such as the near collapse of Long Term Capital Management)."

What Title V does:

Title V creates the Federal Insurance Office (FIO) in the Treasury to monitor the insurance industry, conduct studies, coordinate international insurance matters, and help FSOC identify systemically important insurers.

It makes changes to surplus line insurance and reinsurance regulation.

Why Title V's approach is flawed:

The FIO has largely unconstrained ability to demand information.

Designating insurance companies as systemic aggravates the too-big-to-fail problem and introduces an inexperienced regulator in the insurance space without solving the insurance regulatory failures in evidence at entities like AIG.

TITLE V

Insurance

ITLE V OF Dodd-Frank creates a Federal Insurance Office (FIO) and addresses certain other state insurance-reform issues unrelated to the crisis.[1] The FIO is part of the Treasury Department, and the Treasury secretary appoints its director. As discussed below, the FIO monitors the insurance industry and plays an international coordinating role rather than exercising a direct regulatory role. Under Dodd-Frank, state insurance regulators retain their preeminent role in insurance regulation.[2]

The limited nature of the changes to insurance regulation reflects the fact that the framers of Dodd-Frank did not believe insurance companies were central to the crisis. AIG, of course, was the most notorious exception.[3] Because AIG narratives tend to downplay the role AIG insurance subsidiaries played in the crisis, AIG's failure was blamed largely on the derivatives portfolio at AIG's noninsurance Financial Products unit. In reality, a number of AIG life insurance subsidiaries were dangerously exposed to the residential mortgage market. Without federal government intervention, some of these insurance subsidiaries likely would not have been solvent.[4] Had Dodd-Frank's authors recognized this, they might have included more substantial changes to insurance regulation, including, perhaps, an optional federal charter.[5]

Although the FIO is a relatively modest step toward increased federal government involvement in insurance regulation, the FIO could be the beginning of much more active federal government participation. Indeed, this is what opponents of the FIO fear[6] and others hope will happen.[7] There have long been calls for an optional federal charter as an alternative to the current state-by-state chartering that requires compliance with multiple state-based insurance regulatory regimes.

Even if further changes are not made, the FIO has considerable power in the areas in which it has authority to act. First, the FIO will serve as the representative of the United States in international insurance matters.[8] Especially at a time when there are a lot of international developments in insurance regulation,[9] this is an important role. In conjunction with that role, the FIO has some preemption powers.[10]

Second, the office has the broad authority to require insurance companies and their affiliates "to submit such data or information as the Office may reasonably require in carrying out" its mandates.[11] Among these mandates are monitoring the industry for systemic issues, making recommendations to the FSOC, monitoring the availability of coverage to underserved populations, developing federal policy on international insurance issues, and a catch-all mandate for "other related duties and authorities as may be assigned" by the Treasury secretary.[12] Before approaching insurers directly, the FIO is supposed to rely on other sources of information, including state regulators. Nevertheless, Title V gives court-enforceable subpoena power to the director of the FIO, who is a career employee rather than a politically accountable official.[13]

Third, the FIO has the power to recommend an insurance company to the FSOC for designation as a systemic nonbank financial company to be regulated by the Fed.[14] This recommendation is likely to carry weight with the FSOC and the Treasury secretary, who appoints the director of the FIO and chairs the FSOC. A designation has the potential to change dramatically the manner in which an insurance company is regulated. The ultimate effect of a designation is difficult to predict, but on balance it is likely to improve the competitive position of a designated insurance company, which the market is likely to perceive as too big to fail.

Finally, the FIO will play a central role in the debate over whether and how to reform insurance regulation. One of the FIO's biggest tasks under Title V is the preparation of a report on how to modernize and improve the system of insurance regulation in the United States.[15] This eagerly anticipated report was due in January 2012, 18 months after the passage of Dodd-Frank. As of November 1, 2012, it had not been issued. The FIO put out a brief request for comment last year and has received numerous comment letters.[16] The report, which will likely include legislative, administrative, or regulatory recommendations, could help dictate the next steps in insurance regulatory reform.

Dodd-Frank dipped its toe into increased federalization of insurance regulation. The changes it made were predominantly outgrowths of debates that had begun long before the financial crisis. Title V cannot, therefore, be characterized as a response to the crisis, but it may be the beginning of a dramatic shift in the way insurance is regulated.

NOTES

1. Specifically, Subtitle B of Title V relates to surplus lines and reinsurance issues. Bills introduced in Congress before the crisis included similar language. See Baird Webel, *The Dodd-Frank Wall Street Reform and Consumer Protection Act: Insurance Provisions* (Washington, DC: Congressional Research Service, 2010), 5.

2. The McCarran-Ferguson Act of 1945 reserved insurance regulation for the states. *McCarran-Ferguson Act of 1945, U.S. Code* 15 (1945), §§ 1011 et seq.

3. The failures of monoline bond insurers and the government's capital injection in Hartford Financial Group and Lincoln National Corporation through the Troubled Asset Relief Program were other examples of insurance companies' troubles

during the financial crisis.

4. For an in-depth analysis of the state of AIG's insurance subsidiaries, see David J. Merkel, "To What Degree Were AIG's Operating Insurance Subsidiaries Sound?" April 28, 2009, http://alephblog.com/wp-content/uploads/2009/04/To%20What %20Degree%20Were%20AIG%E2%80%99s%20Operating%20Subsidiaries%20 Sound.pdf.

5. The FSOC could designate insurance companies as systemic under Title I and therefore subject them to regulation by the Fed, which, as a banking regulator, is ill-equipped to regulate insurance companies.

6. See, for example, John D. Doak, "Insurance Oversight Overkill: New Federal Insurance Office Interferes with Efficient State Insurance Regulation," *Washington Times*, November 11, 2011, http://www.washingtontimes.com/news/2011/nov/11 /insurance-oversight-overkill/?page=all#pagebreak. Doak writes, "One needn't be a states' rights alarmist to see the writing on the wall for state insurance departments. The FIO drives a wedge between insurers, policyholders and rightful regulators in each state capital." Doak subsequently called for a review of the constitutionality of the FIO. John D. Doak, Oklahoma Insurance Commissioner, "Doak Asks Attorney Generals to Protect State's Rights against Federal Office of Insurance," news release, March 2, 2012, http://www.ok.gov/triton/modules/newsroom /newsroom_article.php?id=157&article_id=6427.

7. See, for example, Committee on Capital Markets Regulation, letter to Michael T. McRaith, director, FIO, "Public Input on the Report to Congress on How to Modernize and Improve the System of Insurance Regulation in the United States," December 16, 2011, http://www.capmktsreg.org/pdfs/2011.12.16_Insurance_letter .pdf. The letter recommends that the FIO embrace the optional federal charter.

8. *Dodd-Frank Wall Street Reform and Consumer Protection Act,* § 502, adding *U.S. Code* 31, § 313(c)(1)(E).

9. Europe, for example, is in the process of planning the implementation of its Solvency II Directive. One of the important issues is the equivalence of the US regulatory framework.

10. Ibid., adding *U.S. Code* 31, § 313(f). Preemption is possible if the state regulation gives US-domiciled insurance companies an unfair advantage over non-US-domiciled insurers or otherwise violates an international insurance agreement.

11. Ibid., adding *U.S. Code* 31, § 313(e). The FIO has the option of exempting small insurers from information requests.

12. Ibid., adding *U.S. Code 31,* § 313(c).

13. Ibid., adding *U.S. Code* 31, § 313(e)(6).

14. Ibid., adding *U.S. Code* 31, § 313(c)(1)(C). The director of the FIO also serves as a nonvoting member of the FSOC.

15. Ibid., adding *U.S. Code* 31, § 313(p).

16. Department of Treasury, "Public Input on the Report to Congress on How to Modernize and Improve the System of Insurance Regulation in the United States," Notice and Request for Comment, *Federal Register* 76 (2011), 64174. The request for comment essentially restated, and asked for comment on, the statutorily mandated factors for consideration in the study.

What Title VI does:

Title VI expands the Fed's regulatory authority
to include a range of new entities.

It implements the Volcker Rule, which prohibits banks
from engaging in proprietary trading and from involvement
with hedge funds and private equity funds.

Why Title VI's approach is flawed:

Title VI consolidates an inordinate amount of regulatory power
in the Fed, despite the Fed's past regulatory failures.

It increases the likelihood that the Fed and other regulators
will prop up failing financial firms in the future.

Because the statutory language is ambiguous and the
proposed rules are even more so, the Volcker Rule could
make it difficult for banks to engage in legitimate hedging and
market-making activities. Market liquidity could suffer.

TITLE VI
New Authority for the Fed

ITLE VI OF Dodd-Frank, the "Bank and Savings Association Holding Company and Depository Institution Regulatory Improvements Act," makes significant changes with respect to regulation of financial institutions. Some of these changes attempt to respond to issues underlying the financial crisis,[1] but Title VI places renewed trust in, and expands the authority of, the same regulators that failed during the crisis. It also draws arbitrary regulatory lines that will cause the industry to make significant changes, but may not leave the system any more stable.[2]

One area in which the lines have been drawn arbitrarily is in a Title VI provision that has garnered a lot of attention: the so-called Volcker Rule.[3] The prohibition on banks' proprietary trading and involvement with hedge funds and private equity funds was added to Dodd-Frank at the suggestion of Paul Volcker, former chairman of the Fed. Volcker explained the logic behind his idea:

> The basic point is that there has been, and remains, a strong public interest in providing a "safety net"—in particular, deposit insurance and the provision of liquidity in emergencies—for commercial banks carrying out essential services. There is not, however, a similar rationale for public funds—taxpayer funds—protecting and supporting essentially proprietary and speculative activities. Hedge funds, private

equity funds, and trading activities unrelated to customer needs and continuing banking relationships should stand on their own, without the subsidies implied by public support for depository institutions.[4]

The logic of the Volcker Rule is appealing: If the government is going to insure banks, there should be limits on the types of activities in which they engage. Volcker anticipated that translating that simple principle into a workable rule would not be too difficult:

> Every banker I speak with knows very well what "proprietary trading" means and implies. My understanding is that only a handful of large commercial banks—maybe four or five in the United States and perhaps a couple of dozen worldwide—are now engaged in this activity in volume.[5]

Instead, the rule was translated into ambiguous statutory language followed by even more ambiguous proposed rules.[6] Its reach goes far beyond the four or five banks heavily engaged in the offending activity Volcker identified. As for substance, the rule focuses on the intent behind an activity rather than on its risk, so it "forces regulators to peer into the hearts of bankers."[7]

The Volcker Rule could severely affect liquidity and make it difficult for banks to hedge their own risks. Under the rule, the line between permissible market making or hedging on the one hand and proprietary trading on the other is not clear. To avoid running afoul of the prohibition, banks are likely to engage in less legitimate market making and hedging activity than they otherwise would.[8] As an unintended consequence, banks could be less stable as their activities are less diversified and not as adequately hedged. The magnitude of the Volcker Rule's effect depends a great deal on what the final rule looks like and how the regulators exercise their discretion under the rule.[9]

The issue the Volcker Rule set out to solve—preventing safety-net creep—is addressed to some degree by restrictions on transactions between insured depositories and their affiliates, which were considerably tightened under Title VI.[10] Further measures are needed to increase the accountability of firms' creditors and shareholders. A fundamental question is whether depositors and taxpayers are really better off with a system that dulls institutions' incentives to temper their risk taking and forces government regulators to assess whether a particular transaction is an appropriate hedge or an inappropriate pursuit of profit. The Volcker Rule is one example of how the post-Dodd-Frank regulatory system for large banks is rooted in a belief that regulators can stop sophisticated banks from losing money. Large banks are limited in their activities and not permitted to earn excessive profits, but they are also not permitted to lose large amounts of money or to go out of business. The price of a generous safety net for the financial industry may be a public-utility approach to banking regulation, which has negative implications for the quality, price, and availability of banking products and services.

The Fed, despite regulatory failures that contributed to the crisis,[11] was able to retain and expand its powers under Dodd-Frank. The Fed acknowledges some regulatory failures, but contends that it is uniquely positioned, because of its role as a central bank, to be the super-financial regulator:

> The role of the Federal Reserve in a reoriented financial regulatory system derives, in our view, directly from its position as the nation's central bank. Financial stability is integral to the achievement of maximum employment and price stability, the dual mandate that Congress has conferred on the Federal Reserve as its objectives in the conduct of monetary policy. Indeed, there are some important synergies between systemic risk regulation and monetary policy, as insights garnered

from each of those functions informs the performance of the other. Close familiarity with private credit relationships, particularly among the largest financial institutions and through critical payment and settlement systems, makes monetary policy makers better able to anticipate how their actions will affect the economy. Conversely, the substantial economic analysis that accompanies monetary policy decisions can reveal potential vulnerabilities of financial institutions.[12]

The additional grants of authority to the Fed in Title VI are troublesome precisely because of its monetary-policy role. The Fed, accustomed to secrecy and independence from political accountability in its monetary policy, generally makes its rules behind closed doors[13] and without economic analysis.[14] The contention that the Fed's regulatory responsibilities are intertwined with its monetary policy responsibilities could shield those regulatory decisions from scrutiny.[15]

Title VI increases the Fed's power in a number of ways.[16] For example, the Fed is given new authority to conduct supplemental regulation of functionally regulated subsidiaries of bank and thrift holding companies.[17] Thus, the Fed will be able to regulate entities already regulated by the CFTC or SEC. The Fed is given a new, broad factor—stability of the financial system—to consider in reviewing mergers, acquisitions, and consolidations.[18] The Fed, rather than the SEC, is given regulatory authority over broker-dealer holding companies that want a consolidated regulator (typically to satisfy foreign regulatory requirements).[19]

The Fed did not get the same degree of authority with respect to industrial loan companies (ILCs),[20] but Dodd-Frank opens the door to an enhanced Fed role in the future. Title VI places a three-year moratorium on deposit insurance for new commercially owned ILCs to allow the Government Accountability Office (GAO) to study ILCs and for Congress to consider the results of that study.[21] ILCs' record during the financial crisis was relatively good,[22] but ILCs—particularly commercially owned ILCs—had been a subject of debate before the crisis.[23] Bank regulators contend that the same logic that requires holding companies of other financial institutions to be regulated applies to holding companies of ILCs and, moreover, that commercial ownership adds an additional element of risk.[24] Although Title VI laid the groundwork for handing ILC holding companies over to the Fed for regulation,[25] the decision to study the issue before doing so showed relative restraint. This restraint was particularly important given the GAO's finding that, were the Fed to be designated the ILC holding company supervisor, commercial companies would shed their ILCs.[26]

Underlying Title VI is a great deference to the ability of regulators to safeguard the financial system. The title expands regulators' authority over a range of financial companies and activities and allows them great discretion in exercising that authority. With that authority comes responsibility if one of those entities fails. In order to avoid being blamed for missing a structural weakness at a regulated firm, regulators may instead be inclined to take extraordinary steps to prop up failing regulated entities.

NOTES

1. For example, Title VI contains a number of new requirements related to capital and the relationship between insured depositories and affiliates. See, for example, *Dodd-Frank Wall Street Reform and Consumer Protection Act,* § 616, pursuant to which capital requirements will now be countercyclical, rather than procyclical, and holding companies must serve as sources of strength for their insured depository subsidiaries. Provisions unrelated to the crisis, but long overdue, include two that lifted constraints on the banking industry. See *Dodd-Frank Wall Street Reform and Consumer Protection Act,* § 613, which permits de novo branching into states. See also *Dodd-Frank Wall Street Reform and Consumer Protection Act,* § 627, which

lifts the prohibition on paying interest on demand deposits.

2. Moreover, by focusing regulators' attention on activities that are not inherently problematic but nevertheless cross an arbitrary regulatory line, Title VI could facilitate regulatory failure. See, for example, Saule T. Omarova, "The Dodd-Frank Act: A New Deal for a New Age," *North Carolina Banking Institute Journal* 15 (2011): 89, 94. Omarova writes, "Instead of identifying innovative ways to limit upfront the overall level of risk in the system, Congress chose to rely on the familiar technique of creating statutory firewalls around depository institutions, based on formalistic and inherently static criteria and an over-simplified concept of risk transfer."

3. *Dodd-Frank Wall Street Reform and Consumer Protection Act,* § 619.

4. Senate Committee on Banking, Housing, and Urban Affairs, *Prohibiting Certain High-Risk Investment Activities by Banks and Bank Holding Companies,* 111th Cong., 2d Sess. (Feb. 2, 2010) (statement of Paul A. Volcker), 1–2, http://banking.senate .gov/public/index.cfm?FuseAction=Files.View&FileStore_id=ec787c56-dbd2 -4498-bbbd-ddd23b58c1c4.

5. Ibid., 3.

6. The regulators issued two similar proposals, one by the CFTC and the other by the SEC and the banking regulators. CFTC, "Prohibitions and Restrictions on Proprietary Trading and Certain Interests in, and Relationships with, Hedge Funds and Covered Funds," Notice of Proposed Rulemaking, *Federal Register* 77 (February 14, 2012), 8332; OCC et al., "Prohibitions and Restrictions on Proprietary Trading and Certain Interests in, and Relationships with, Hedge Funds and Private Equity Funds," Notice of Proposed Rulemaking, *Federal Register* 76 (November 7, 2011), 68846. They have yet to finalize a rule, despite the fact that the statutory deadline for adoption has passed. The Volcker Rule is automatically effective, even without the finalization of the rules. The regulators provided a measure of relief by extending the period for conformance with the Volcker Rule but directing entities to engage in "good faith conformance efforts" in the interim. Board of Governors of the Fed, "Statement of Policy Regarding the Conformance Period for Entities Engaged in Prohibited Proprietary Trading or Private Equity Fund or Hedge Fund Activities," Notice of Policy Statement, *Federal Register* 77 (June 8, 2012), 33,949, 33,950. Characteristic of much of the Volcker Rule process, this statement has led to a fair amount of uncertainty about what regulators' expectations are pending finalization of a rule.

7. House Financial Services Committee, *The Volcker Rule and Its Impact on the U.S. Economy,* 112th Cong., 2d sess., January 18, 2012 (statement of Douglas J. Elliott), http://www.brookings.edu/research/testimony/2012/01/18-volcker-rule-elliott.

8. Some regulators would like the rules to be even less accommodative of hedging and market-making activities. See, for example, Sarah Bloom Raskin, governor, Fed, "How Well Is Our Financial System Serving Us? Working Together to Find the

High Road" (speech, Graduate School of Banking at Colorado, Boulder, CO, July 23, 2012), http://www.federalreserve.gov/newsevents/speech/raskin20120723a .htm. Raskin says, "It is not inconceivable to think that the potential costs associated with permitting hedging and market-making within these exemptions still outweigh the benefits we as a society supposedly receive from permitting these capital market activities. The potential compliance, supervisory, and other costs could be so great as to eliminate whatever value may arguably be derived by virtue of these capital market activities."

9. The regulators are given broad authority to require an entity covered by the rule to stop an activity or dispose of an investment whenever a regulator believes the entity is trying to evade the requirements of the Volcker Rule.

10. *Dodd-Frank Wall Street Reform and Consumer Protection Act*, §§ 608 and 609, which amend §§ 23A and 23B(e) of the *Federal Reserve Act, U. S. Code* 12 (December 1913), §§ 371c and 371c-1(e).

11. See, for example, GAO, "Characteristics and Regulation of Exempt Institutions and the Implications of Removing the Exemptions" (GAO Report 12-160, Washington, DC, January 2012), 43. The report states, "Federal Reserve officials acknowledged that consolidated supervision needed to be improved in light of the financial problems experienced by several bank holding companies during the 2007–2009 financial crisis but noted that they had learned many lessons from the crisis."

12. US House Committee on Financial Services, *Regulatory Restructuring*, 111th Cong., 1st sess., July 24, 2009 (statement of Ben S. Bernanke), http://www.federal reserve.gov/newsevents/testimony/bernanke20090724a.htm.

13. The Fed does not generally conduct its meetings regarding rulemaking in public, despite a policy statement that provides public meetings should be the norm. See Fed, "Statement of Policy Regarding Expanded Rulemaking Procedures," Statement of Policy, *Federal Register* 44 (1979), 3957, 3958.

14. See Office of Inspector General of the Fed, *Response to a Congressional Request Regarding the Economic Analysis Associated with Specific Rulemakings* (Washington, DC, June 2011), 6, http://www.federalreserve.gov/oig/files/Congressional_Re sponse_web.pdf. The response states, "A number of key statutes related to the Board's regulatory authority, including the Federal Reserve Act and the Bank Holding Company Act of 1956, provide the Board with rulemaking authority to perform the duties, functions, or services specified in these statutes. These statutes generally do not require economic analysis as part of the agency's rulemaking activities."

15. The issue of Fed transparency is discussed in detail in the section on Title XI.

16. Title VI, however, also constrains the Fed's power in some limited ways. For example, the restrictions on affiliated transactions under sections 23A and 23B of the Federal Reserve Act are tightened, and the Fed's ability to provide exemptions is now more limited than it was prior to Dodd-Frank. See *Dodd-Frank Wall Street*

Reform and Consumer Protection Act, §§ 608 and 609. Another limit on the Fed is the back-up authority other federal banking agencies are given to examine the activities of certain subsidiaries of depository institution holding companies if the Fed fails to do so as required under Title VI. *Dodd-Frank Wall Street Reform and Consumer Protection Act,* § 605(a). The examining federal banking agency can assess the examined subsidiary for the costs of an examination under this provision.

17. Ibid., § 604.

18. Ibid., § 604(d) and § 604(e). Subsection 604(d) adds the requirement to consider an increase or concentration of "risks to the stability of the United States banking or financial system" in connection with bank acquisitions. Subsection 604(e) adds a requirement to consider "risk to the stability of the United States banking or financial system" in connection with nonbank acquisitions. The Fed has subsequently explained how it will exercise this authority:

> To assess the likelihood that failure of the resulting firm may inflict material damage on the broader economy, the Board will consider a variety of metrics. These would include measures of the size of the resulting firm; availability of substitute providers for any critical products and services offered by the resulting firm; interconnectedness of the resulting firm with the banking or financial system; extent to which the resulting firm contributes to the complexity of the financial system; and extent of the cross-border activities of the resulting firm. These categories are not exhaustive, and additional categories could inform the Board's decision. . . . In addition to these quantitative measures, the Board will consider qualitative factors, such as the opaqueness and complexity of an institution's internal organization, that are indicative of the relative degree of difficulty of resolving the resulting firm.

Fed, "Capital One Financial Corporation: Order Approving the Acquisition of a Savings Association and Nonbanking Subsidiaries" (FRB Order No. 2012-2, Washington, DC, February 14, 2012), 28–30, http://www.federalreserve.gov/newsevents/press/orders/order20120214.pdf. Title VI also imposes concentration limits on large firms but gives the Fed latitude to waive those under certain circumstances. See *Dodd-Frank Wall Street Reform and Consumer Protection Act,* § 622.

19. *Dodd-Frank Wall Street Reform and Consumer Protection Act,* § 618. The Fed has stated that, at the beginning at least, broker-dealer holding companies ("securities holding companies") will be treated similarly to bank holding companies: "Supervised securities holding companies will, among other things, be required to submit the same reports and be subject to the same examination procedures, supervisory guidance, and capital standards that currently apply to bank holding

companies." Fed, "Supervised Securities Holding Company Registration," Notice of Final Rulemaking, *Federal Register* 77 (June 4, 2012), 32881–82. Dodd-Frank gave the Fed broad discretion to determine how to regulate securities holding companies.

20. ILCs provide banking services, but their parent companies are exempt from the Bank Holding Company Act, which means the Fed is not the consolidated supervisor for the parent entity and the activity restrictions applicable to bank holding companies do not apply. Depository ILCs, however, are insured and regulated by the FDIC.

21. *Dodd-Frank Wall Street Reform and Consumer Protection Act,* § 603. In addition to ILCs, other companies that operate under an exemption from the Bank Holding Company Act were included in the moratorium and GAO study. The study was completed in January 2012. GAO, "Characteristics and Regulation of Exempt Institutions and the Implications of Removing the Exemptions," Report 12-160.

22. As of June 30, 2011, there were 34 ILCs, and there were 2 ILC failures between 2007 and 2010. GAO, "Characteristics and Regulation of Exempt Institutions and the Implications of Removing the Exemptions," Report 12-160, 15, 30.

23. In particular, several years before the crisis, concerns were raised over ILCs owned by nonfinancial companies when Wal-Mart and other commercial companies attempted to start ILCs. Proponents of ILCs and commercial ownership thereof argue that ILCs are strong institutions and commercial companies are a valuable source of capital for ILCs. For a discussion of these points and, more generally, a thorough discussion of the history, characteristics, and benefits of ILCs, see James R. Barth and Tong Li, "Industrial Loan Companies: Supporting America's Financial System," (Milken Institute, April 2011), http://www.business.auburn.edu/~barthjr/publications/Industrial%20Loan%20Companies%20Supporting%20America_s%20Financial%20System.pdf.

24. For a discussion of regulators' concerns and commercial ILCs' rejoinders, see GAO, "Characteristics and Regulation of Exempt Institutions and the Implications of Removing the Exemptions," Report 12-160.

25. The Fed told the GAO that "if the exemption were not removed and the Dodd-Frank moratorium expired, the number and size of ILCs could grow to the much higher levels that they had reached prior to the financial crisis." Ibid., 44. If this prediction came to pass, the Fed could try to reach ILCs through a systemic designation under Title I of Dodd-Frank.

26. Ibid., 33. The GAO found, however, there would be only "a limited impact on the overall credit market." Ibid., 36.

What Title VII does:

Title VII assigns regulatory responsibility for the over-the-counter (OTC) derivatives market to the CFTC and SEC.

It reshapes the OTC derivatives market by mandating reporting of transactions to regulators and the public, mandating the use of central clearinghouses, forcing swaps to trade on exchanges, and closely regulating dealer-customer interactions.

Why Title VII's approach is flawed:

Title VII fragments regulation of OTC derivatives markets by assigning responsibility to two regulatory agencies.

It imposes a regulatory scheme that better suits a highly liquid retail market.

It impedes the ability of companies, farmers, utilities, and others to manage their risks efficiently and cost-effectively.

It does not sufficiently take into account that a financially weak or poorly managed OTC derivatives clearinghouse could exacerbate systemic risk in the financial system.

Regulators' overly aggressive, uncoordinated, and inadequately analyzed approach to implementation increases the likelihood that new rules will have harmful unintended effects.

TITLE VII

Derivatives

T ITLE VII OF Dodd-Frank creates an elaborate new regulatory structure for the over-the-counter (OTC) derivatives market.[1] Title VII grew out of the realization that regulators and market participants lacked a thorough understanding of the very large and important OTC derivatives market, which complicated their ability to respond to the crisis.[2] Title VII attempts, however, to reshape the OTC derivatives market so it looks like the highly liquid equities and futures markets with exchange trading and retail participants.[3] In the process, changes under Title VII will undermine the risk-management ability of companies, municipalities, farmers, utilities, and others that have successfully used OTC derivatives in the past to manage their business risks.[4] Moreover, the focus on fundamentally reforming the market has hampered efforts to improve market transparency for regulators.

The implementation of Title VII by the CFTC—which is charged with regulating the vast majority of the OTC derivatives market—and the SEC is likely to intensify, rather than moderate, the damaging effects of Title VII. First, the failure of the regulators to work effectively with one another by, for example, failing to coordinate the timing and content of similar rules, adds an unnecessary layer of confusion to the implementation process and makes international coordination more difficult.[5] Second, the failure of the regulators to undertake rigorous economic analysis of their actions has made it even more likely that the Title VII regime will have harmful effects.

OTC derivatives, or "swaps,"[6] are used by banks, pension plans, insurance companies, commercial companies, and others to transfer or hedge risk. Swaps are used to manage exposure to foreign exchange–rate, interest-rate, and commodity-price fluctuations and to hedge counterparty credit risk. For accounting and business reasons, many swaps are closely tailored to the precise risk a company faces.[7] These tailored swaps are generally bilateral transactions between a swap dealer and its customer. Depending on the nature of the risk being managed, these swaps can remain in place for days, weeks, months, or years. For less-precise risk management, exchange-traded futures contracts are often used. The dealers who offer swaps also use swaps to hedge and transfer their own risks to other dealers.

Title VII attempts to do too much to change the swaps markets and does not achieve its central objectives effectively. The primary objectives are increased regulatory transparency, increased public transparency, mandated central clearing, mandated exchange-like trading, and enhanced customer protection.

First, Title VII requires that data about swaps transactions be available to regulators. Regulators, during the crisis, did not have an accurate and complete understanding of the swaps market, so efforts to improve the information available to them are commendable. Information about swaps transactions will be transmitted to and retained by Swap Data Repositories (SDRs), which will have to be registered with either the CFTC or the SEC.

Dodd-Frank undermines its own regulatory transparency efforts through its indemnification provisions. The indemnification provisions effectively prevent information sharing among regulators by prohibiting an SDR from sharing information with a domestic or international regulator other than the commission with which it is registered, absent an agreement "to indemnify the [SDR] and [the commission with which it is registered] for any expenses arising from litigation relating to the information provided."[8] The SEC has called for the removal of the provision, partly on the grounds that its existence in Dodd-Frank has sparked European efforts to take retaliatory measures.[9] Removing the indemnification provisions would facilitate international and domestic regulators' access to information about the swaps markets.

Second, swap transactions will have to be publicly reported. With respect to standardized and heavily traded categories of swaps, greater public transparency can be expected to lower prices for dealers' customers.[10] With respect to customized and infrequently traded categories of swaps, however, public reporting could adversely affect the ability of companies to hedge their risks; dealers will be hesitant to enter into a transaction if they have to report it before they are able to hedge their resulting position. If the transparency rules and exceptions from those rules are not properly calibrated, market participants' business strategies could be compromised and market liquidity could be harmed.[11] It is important not to view the swaps market as a monolith to which the rules of the very liquid, standardized equities and futures markets can be applied. The swaps rules must be flexible enough to accommodate the broad range of categories of swaps, some of which are highly standardized and widely traded[12] and others of which trade only infrequently or are uniquely tailored to a particular customer's risks.

Third, Title VII champions central clearing of swaps. This objective reflects a concern that swaps transactions, many of which are long-dated, create dangerous cross-exposures among financial-market participants. In a time of crisis, the failure of one of those participants would transmit rapidly to the rest of the market through these swap interconnections. Central clearing is Dodd-Frank's answer to this potential problem. Once a transaction is executed, it gets moved to a central clearinghouse, which steps in as the new counterparty to each of the original parties to the transaction. If a large swap dealer fails, the central counterparty muffles the effect on other market participants. Central clearinghouses have proved useful in the futures and options markets and are beneficial in the swaps context, but they are not immune from trouble.[13] Centrally clearing complex swaps effectively and safely is much more difficult than centrally clearing plain-vanilla futures and options. Understanding and managing the risks of and correlations among different types of swaps is difficult.

Dodd-Frank does not take sufficient account of the possibility that a financially weak or poorly managed clearinghouse could falter and devastate the financial markets.[14] In fact, Dodd-Frank's Title VII requirements could destabilize clearinghouses. Well-meaning attempts to quickly move as many swaps as possible into clearinghouses could bring unmanaged risks into clearinghouses.[15] Clearinghouses, encouraged by regulators eager for the proliferation of clearing, could undertake to clear swaps without fully comprehending their risk characteristics and, as a consequence, they may not impose adequate margin requirements. Regulations dictating the standards for clearinghouse membership and governance likewise can have the unintended consequences of increasing the level of risks to which clearinghouses are exposed and weakening the clearinghouses' ability to prudently manage those risks. In implementing Title VII, regulators have acknowledged that a clearinghouse could be a systemic risk[16] but have favored regulatory approaches that threaten effective risk management, such as weakening membership requirements for clearinghouses.

The fourth objective of Title VII is to force swaps to trade on exchanges or exchange-like facilities called "Swap Execution Facilities" (SEFs). Dodd-Frank left the definition of the contours of SEFs to the regulators. In contrast to the SEC's approach, the CFTC's approach, which many contend is not consistent with Dodd-Frank's statutory language, is inflexible as to permissible methods of execution.[17] As commissioner Scott O'Malia explains,

The entire market from buy-side asset managers, pension funds, commercial end-users, farm credit banks and rural power cooperatives to sell-side dealers and even prospective SEFs expressed concern that if the final rules are adopted as proposed, market participants will be restricted in their ability to obtain price discovery because the proposed SEF rules would limit their choice of execution.[18]

Exchange-like trading is appropriate for some swaps, but others are illiquid, and forcing them to trade in this manner could further constrain liquidity or prevent them from trading altogether.

The final objective of Dodd-Frank is to protect customers, a goal that reflects understandable concern about the concentration of the swaps market in the hands of a small number of large swap dealers. Swaps markets, however, are not retail markets; they are limited to sophisticated parties capable of choosing—or hiring someone to choose—the products, counterparties, and execution venues that best serve them.[19] Remaking the market under Dodd-Frank may harm the entities regulators think they are helping.

Some customers, by virtue of broad regulatory definitions, may find themselves categorized as swap dealers or major swap participants, a status that will subject them to the clearing mandate and all of the other requirements designed for dealers. Others will find themselves unable to rely on the end-user exemption from clearing.[20] Even those able to rely on the end-user exemption from clearing are likely to face very expensive margin requirements.[21] They may conclude that avoiding swaps and leaving their commercial risk unhedged is preferable to tying up large amounts of cash in order to margin swaps.

Dodd-Frank also establishes an elaborate set of business conduct rules—in some cases more prescriptive than retail-market rules—to protect swap customers. The most stringent requirements apply to transactions with "special entities," which include government agencies, employee benefit plans, and endowments.[22] Users of swaps will face additional, and often unnecessary, hurdles or expenses as they seek to enter into swap transactions.[23]

Title VII is not only problematic because of what it does but also because of what it does not do. Even before Dodd-Frank, many observers believed the CFTC and SEC should be merged.[24] The CFTC's purview had grown beyond futures on agricultural commodities to include many financial futures, and jurisdictional disputes between the SEC and CFTC were common.[25] Dodd-Frank further complicated matters by dividing jurisdiction over the OTC derivatives market between the two agencies along an awkwardly drawn line of demarcation.[26] As a consequence, the two agencies are engaged in duplicative rule-writing exercises, and market participants will have to comply with two sometimes inconsistent sets of regulations. Had Dodd-Frank merged the SEC and CFTC, or at least set up a cross-agency unit for the purpose of overseeing the swaps market, it would have been a meaningful step toward simplifying US financial regulatory structure. Instead, Dodd-Frank perpetuated and deepened the regulatory divide.

Dodd-Frank's approach to remaking the swaps market may end up harming the users of swaps it is purportedly designed to help and may compromise the stability of the financial system. Piling swaps into central clearinghouses may set these entities and, as a consequence, our financial system, up for a fall. Further, costly changes may cause swap end users to hedge fewer of their risks and new rules may cause some swap dealers to exit the market, thus further reducing competition. Title VII, with its limitations on regulatory access to data, may not even enable regulators to get the information they need to monitor the markets.

NOTES

1. Derivatives are financial instruments that derive their value by reference to something else, such as a commodity, an interest rate, or a bond. While some types of derivatives trade on exchanges, OTC derivatives transactions are privately negotiated between two parties.

2. Much is made of the fact that the OTC derivatives market was largely unregulated, but its biggest participants are heavily regulated banks, and their derivatives activities were not beyond the purview of regulators.

3. Title VII makes other changes that are beyond the scope of this chapter. Some of these provisions, such as the considerable expansion of the CFTC's enforcement powers, are having effects beyond the OTC derivatives markets.

4. See, for example, Scott O'Malia, commissioner, CFTC, "Stifling the Swaps Markets before Dodd-Frank Rules Take Effect" (speech, European Federation of Energy Traders Deutschland, Parliamentary Evening: Market Transparency and Supervision, September 27, 2012), http://www.cftc.gov/PressRoom/SpeechesTestimony/opaomalia-18. O'Malia says, "Despite the fact that derivatives end-users did not contribute to the financial crisis, they are now forced to follow ambiguous and inconsistent rules. I am concerned that imposition of unnecessary regulations on end-users will create more economic instability and will impede U.S. competitiveness in the global market."

5. See, for example, Jill E. Sommers, commissioner, CFTC, "Remarks before the Institute of International Bankers" (speech, Institute of International Bankers Annual Washington Conference, Washington, DC, March 5, 2012), http://www.cftc.gov/PressRoom/SpeechesTestimony/opasommers-21. Sommers notes the importance of a consistent approach by the SEC and CFTC to extraterritorial application of Dodd-Frank and worries that "there has not been adequate coordination with the SEC and the international regulatory community."

6. Title VII separates the OTC derivatives that it regulates into two primary categories: swaps and security-based swaps. The former are regulated by the CFTC, and the latter are regulated by the SEC. For simplicity's sake, this book uses the term "swaps" to refer to both categories. Neither term was defined completely in the statute. Instead, Dodd-Frank directed the SEC and CFTC to further define those and other key terms in Title VII. Regulators waited until two years after the passage of Dodd-Frank to define key terms. CFTC and SEC, "Further Definition of 'Swap,' 'Security-Based Swap,' and 'Security-Based Swap Agreement'; Mixed Swaps; Security-Based Swap Agreement Recordkeeping," Notice of Final Rulemaking, *Federal Register* 77 (August 13, 2012), 48208. Not knowing the contours of these key terms has made it difficult for commenters to assess other swaps rulemakings,

all of which rely on those terms.

7. The treasurer of a producer of crop-protection chemicals gave the following example of a customized swap: In dealing with Brazilian soybean farmers, the American company sells its "agricultural chemicals for use at planting time in exchange
for an agreed quantity of soybeans at harvest time. We can do this because we
simultaneously enter into a custom OTC derivative that offsets the amount and
timing of the future delivery of soybeans by our customers." House Committee
on Agriculture, Subcommittee on General Farm Commodities and Risk Management, *Harmonizing Global Derivatives Reform: Impact on U.S. Competitiveness and
Market Stability*, 112th Cong., 1st sess., May 25, 2011 (statement of Thomas C. Deas,
FMC Corporation), 2, http://agriculture.house.gov/sites/republicans.agriculture
.house.gov/files/pdf/hearings/Deas110525.pdf.

8. See *Dodd-Frank Wall Street Reform and Consumer Protection Act,* §§ 728, adding
7 U.S.C. § 24a(d), and 763(i), adding 15 U.S.C. § 78m(n). See also *Dodd-Frank Wall
Street Reform and Consumer Protection Act,* § 725, adding 7 U.S.C. § 7a-1(k)(5), an
indemnification provision covering derivatives clearing organizations.

9. For a discussion of the issue, see House Subcommittee on Capital Markets and Government Sponsored Enterprises, *Testimony Concerning Indemnification of Security-Based Swap Data Repositories,* 112th Cong., 2d sess., March 21, 2012 (statement
of Ethiopis Tafara), http://www.sec.gov/news/testimony/2012/ts032112et.htm.

10. Here the experience with the Trade Reporting and Compliance Engine (TRACE)
in the corporate bond market is instructive. See, for example, Amy K. Edwards,
Lawrence E. Harris, and Michael S. Piwowar, "Corporate Bond Market Transaction Costs and Transparency," *Journal of Finance* 3 (2007): 1421. The authors find
that transaction costs fell with increased transparency in corporate bond markets.

11. For example, most swap transactions will be subject to a real-time public-dissem-
ination requirement. See *Commodity Exchange Act, U.S. Code* 7 (1936), § 2(a)(13)
(A) and *Securities Exchange Act, U.S. Code* 15 (1934), § 13(m)(1)(A). The acts define
"real-time public reporting" as "as soon as technologically practicable after the
time at which the [swap/security-based swap] transaction has been executed."
Because certain block trades will be subject to reporting delays, determining what
size trade qualifies as a block trade is important. See, for example, "5 Questions:
What the CFTC's New Block Trading Proposal Means for the Swaps Market; Q&A
with Jeffrey L. Steiner of Gibson, Dunn & Crutcher," *DerivAlert Blog,* May 14, 2012,
http://www.derivalert.org/blog/bid/78078/5-Questions-What-the-CFTC-s-New-
Block-Trading-Proposal-Means-for-the-Swaps-Market. Steiner explains, "If block
trade sizes are set too high, it is possible that the immediate public dissemination
of a swap that has a very large notional amount but is not quite at the appropriate
minimum block size, may enable other market participants to react on that information, making it difficult and more costly for the counterparty to the large swap

to lay off the risk generated from such swap. This potential scenario may be a particular concern for less liquid products within a swap category that may not have as much trading as other products with more liquidity. Accordingly, liquidity may dry up and it may become extremely costly to enter into such products and certain market participants may choose not to offer such products. Additional costs may then be passed on to end-users and ultimately to consumers. On the other hand, if block sizes are set too low, a certain amount of pre-trade and post-trade market transparency may be lost. Increased pre-trade transparency may help to generate liquidity on electronic trading systems or platform, while increased post-trade transparency could increase the amount of information available to the public to enhance price discovery."

12. For highly standardized and heavily traded products, market participants may forgo burdensome swap rules and opt for the less onerous and more familiar futures model. Thus, IntercontinentalExchange (ICE) recently announced that it would convert all of its cleared OTC energy products to futures: "Based upon our extensive analysis of new swap rules and consultations with a wide variety of customers, we believe that these policies will increase the cost and complexity for swaps market participants, both in absolute terms and relative to that of futures market participants." ICE, "IntercontinentalExchange to Transition Cleared Energy Swaps to Futures in January 2013," news release, July 30, 2012, http://ir.theice.com/re leasedetail.cfm?ReleaseID=696379. See also O'Malia, "Stifling the Swaps Markets before Dodd-Frank Rules Take Effect." O'Malia says, "Given the inconsistency in the Commission's interpretation of its own rules, the lack of regulatory certainty and the increased cost of compliance with the Commission swaps regulations, including the complicated and controversial swap dealer definition rules, swap customers have turned to futures markets for regulatory certainty."

13. See, for example, Ben Bernanke, "Clearinghouses, Financial Stability, and Financial Reform" (speech, Financial Markets Conference, Stone Mountain, GA, April 4, 2011), http://www.federalreserve.gov/newsevents/speech/bernanke20110404a .htm. Bernanke explained, "Clearinghouses around the world generally performed well in the highly stressed financial environment of the recent crisis. However, we should not take for granted that we will be as lucky in the future."

14. Professor Craig Pirrong has written extensively about central clearing and the potential attendant risks. See, for example, Craig Pirrong, "The Inefficiency of Clearing Mandates," Cato Policy Analysis, no. 665 (July 21, 2010), http://www.cato.org /pubs/pas/PA665.pdf.

15. Central clearing is appropriate only for swaps that are sufficiently standardized and liquid. Much of the push for central clearing derives from concerns about what happened at AIG, which maintained a large portfolio of unhedged credit default swaps. Given the highly customized nature of these swaps, they would not

have been acceptable for central clearing.

16. See, for example, CFTC, "Derivatives Clearing Organization General Provisions and Core Principles," Notice of Final Rulemaking, *Federal Register* 76 (November 8, 2011), 69334 and 69409, http://www.cftc.gov/ucm/groups/public/@lrfederalregister/documents/file/2011-27536a.pdf. The rulemaking notice acknowledges that "if a [clearinghouse] itself fails or suffers a risk of failure, the consequences for the market at large are likely to be serious and widespread."

17. CFTC, "Core Principles and Other Requirements for Swap Execution Facilities," Notice of Proposed Rulemaking, *Federal Register* 76 (January 27, 2011), 1214.

18. O'Malia, "Stifling the Swaps Markets before Dodd-Frank Rules Take Effect."

19. Some municipalities have experienced notorious losses on interest-rate swaps. As with any risk-management tool, swaps should be employed judiciously.

20. See, for example, O'Malia, "Stifling the Swaps Markets before Dodd-Frank Rules Take Effect." O'Malia remarked, "As adopted, the end-user exception is confusing and defeats the very reason for its existence, which is to allow end-users to mitigate their commercial risk."

21. Dodd-Frank requires regulators to adopt rules "imposing . . . both initial and variation margin requirements on all swaps that are not cleared" in order to "offset the greater risk to the swap dealer or major swap participant and the financial system arising from the use of" uncleared swaps. *Dodd-Frank Wall Street Reform and Consumer Protection Act,* § 731, adding *U.S. Code* 7, § 6s(e). The stringency of the margin requirements on uncleared swaps remains uncertain because rules, which must be adopted by multiple regulators and coordinated internationally, have not yet been finalized. Historically, in hedging transactions with commercial end users, swap dealers have neither posted nor required margin or have exhibited flexibility with respect to the type of margin collected.

22. See, for example, *Dodd-Frank Wall Street Reform and Consumer Protection Act,* § 731, adding *U.S. Code* 7, § 6s(h)(5), which requires swap dealers and major swap participants, when dealing with special entities, "to have a reasonable basis to believe" that the special entity is represented by an independent and knowledgeable representative. These special entities may not be able to enter into swap transactions that would be beneficial to them. See, for example, Jill E. Sommers, "Opening Statement, Eighth Open Meeting to Consider Final Rules, Pursuant to the Dodd-Frank Act" (speech, January 11, 2012), http://www.cftc.gov/PressRoom/SpeechesTestimony/sommersstatement011112. Sommers explained, "Shortly after our proposed rules were published, special entities began to tell us that the protections we proposed were not protections at all. We heard over and over again from special entities, right up until last week, that our rules would not provide additional protections, but would actually harm them by making it more difficult for them to enter into arms-length transactions with swap dealers."

23. The final business-conduct rules adopted by the CFTC are less onerous than those originally proposed, but the new requirements are nevertheless costly to swaps customers and difficult for dealers to implement. See, for example, Jill E. Sommers, "Opening Statement, Eighth Open Meeting to Consider Final Rules." Sommers worries that the CFTC's "so-called protections would actually harm" the entities they were intended to help. The CFTC delayed the compliance date, but market participants are still likely to have trouble meeting the new deadlines. For a discussion of the delay and implementation difficulties, see Lukas Becker, "Despite Extension, Banks Still Fretting over CFTC's Business Conduct Rules," *Risk .net,* September 6, 2012, http://www.risk.net/risk-magazine/feature/2200992/de spite-extension-banks-still-fretting-over-cftcs-business-conduct-rules.

24. A merger would be difficult for political reasons; the two agencies do not share a common oversight committee. The same regulatory efficiency and consistency reasons that support a merger argue for common congressional oversight. Opposition to a merger of the two agencies, however, is sometimes grounded in a belief that competition among regulators is good for markets and allows for innovation that otherwise would not occur. For an argument against a merger of the SEC and CFTC, see Bart Chilton, "Let's Not 'Dial M for Merger'" (speech, Futures Industry Association, Law and Compliance Luncheon, New York, NY, November 13, 2007), http:// www.cftc.gov/PressRoom/SpeechesTestimony/opachilton-4. Chilton explained, "The CFTC has already adopted a principles-based regulatory approach that allows innovation and competition to flourish without undue regulatory impediments and get products to market faster. Its regulatory system is an example of the solution, not the problem. The SEC, on the other hand, is an example of the classic, old-style, prescriptive regulator, and the difference between our two systems shows why it would be such a mistake to merge the SEC and the CFTC. Why would you want to merge an agency with a system that is working well, fostering innovation and competition, with another agency with a fundamentally different mandate?" Chilton later expressed a willingness to revisit the propriety of a merger in light of the financial crisis. Bart Chilton, "Statement of Bart Chilton Regarding CFTC/SEC Merger" (speech, October 28, 2008), http://www.cftc.gov/PressRoom/Speeches Testimony/chiltonstatement102808.

25. For a discussion of some of these jurisdictional disputes, see Wendy L. Gramm and Gerald D. Gay, "Scam, Scoundrels, and Scapegoats: A Taxonomy of CEA Regulation over Derivative Instruments," *Journal of Derivatives* (Spring 1994): 6–24.

26. Additional potential jurisdictional conflicts could come from a number of Dodd-Frank definitions of regulated persons, such as commodity pool operator, floor broker, floor trader, futures commission merchant, and introducing broker. These definitions include a clause that permits the CFTC great latitude in defining the limits of its own jurisdiction. The post-Dodd-Frank CFTC has displayed

a penchant for expanding its jurisdictional reach. See, for example, *Investment Company Institute and Chamber of Commerce of the USA v. CFTC*, complaint (D.D.C. Case No. 1:12-cv-00612). The complaint argues that FTC required certain SEC-regulated advisers to register with the CFTC without demonstrating the inadequacy of SEC regulation.

What Title VIII does:

Title VIII charges the FSOC with designating financial market utilities and payment, clearing, or settlement activities that are, or are likely to become, systemically important.

It grants the Fed, the SEC, and the CFTC new authority to prescribe risk-management standards for designated utilities and firms engaged in designated activities.

It allows the Fed to give discount and borrowing privileges to financial market utilities in an emergency.

Why Title VIII's approach is flawed:

Title VIII creates a new class of too-big-to-fail entities and expands the range of entities able to look to the government for help in times of trouble.

It gives rise to moral hazard through the "provision of ex post insurance" to clearinghouses.

It gives regulators broad, unconstrained regulatory power over firms engaged in designated activities.

TITLE VIII
Systemically Important Utilities and Activities

ITLE VIII—WHICH GIVES regulators broad new authorities over financial market utilities (such as clearinghouses and electronic-payment systems) and companies that engage in payment, clearing, or settlement activities—deserves more attention than it has received. This portion of Dodd-Frank deals with the tremendously important "plumbing" of the financial system. However, as with much of the rest of Dodd-Frank, infused in its approach is deferential reliance on regulators and an expectation that the Fed is the insurer of last resort of the financial system.

The FSOC is charged with designating "financial market utilities or payment, clearing, or settlement activities that the Council determines are, or are likely to become, systemically important."[1] Although most of the attention on Title VIII has been on utility designations, the activity designation portion of the title could end up being a far-reaching regulatory tool. Systemic importance means that the failure of or disruption to the utility or activity "could create, or increase, the risk of significant liquidity or credit problems spreading among financial institutions or markets and thereby threaten the stability of the financial system of the United States."[2]

Entities that are designated or that engage in activities that are designated are subject to heightened oversight. Title VIII directs the

Fed to prescribe risk-management standards for designated utilities and financial institutions carrying out designated activities.[3] The power to prescribe risk-management standards belongs to the SEC and CFTC for their regulated entities.[4] These entities are subject to broad examinations and enforcement actions for violations of Title VIII.[5] The Fed and the FSOC also may impose recordkeeping and reporting requirements on these entities.[6]

To date, the FSOC has not designated any systemically important *activities.*[7] The FSOC's power to do so, which will undoubtedly be exercised at some point, is an example of Dodd-Frank's broad delegations to regulators.[8] Using this power, the FSOC can reach banks, credit unions, investment companies, insurance companies, investment advisers, futures commission merchants, commodity trading advisors, commodity pool operators, and any other "company engaged in activities that are financial in nature or incidental to a financial activity."[9] Once the FSOC designates an activity as systemically important or likely to become systemically important, any entity that engages in any amount of this activity is subject to regulation by the Fed, the SEC, or the CFTC. These regulators may, but need not, set a threshold level of activity such that companies engaged in only a de minimis amount of the designated activity need not comply with the special regulatory standards.[10] In other words, the Fed, the SEC, or the CFTC, with a two-thirds vote of the FSOC, can regulate any company that has any connection to a financial activity. The Fed, SEC, and CFTC have broad latitude with respect to the scope of regulations they may prescribe under this authority.

The FSOC has designated a set of financial market *utilities* as systemic.[11] Once a financial market utility is designated, the Fed can open an account for it, provide payment services like those available to a depository bank, and, in times of emergency, can give it access to the discount window.[12] Thus, Title VIII expands the range of entities able to look to the Fed for help in times of trouble.

Clearinghouses were among the first set of utilities designated by the FSOC. Given Dodd-Frank's push in Title VII for more central clearing of OTC derivatives and the complex nature of the products, OTC derivatives clearinghouses will need to be monitored closely. Prior to the crisis, the Fed had a much stronger interest than the CFTC or SEC in clearinghouse risk management. Therefore, Title VIII, in recognition of the danger that a clearinghouse could pose if it fails, facilitates Fed involvement in clearinghouse risk management.[13]

As mentioned above, however, Title VIII also allows the Fed to step in with emergency assistance if a clearinghouse experiences trouble. Before becoming Fed chairman, Ben S. Bernanke wrote on the role of the government as a backstop in connection with clearing and settlement troubles that arose during the 1987 financial crisis:

> We think that it is certainly possible that much more serious problems could have emerged than actually did [during the 1987 crisis], so luck was with us in that respect. On the other hand, (1) an optimal system is not necessarily a foolproof system and (2) the system, when thought of as including the banking system and the Fed, did not perform so badly. Since it now appears that the Fed is firmly committed to respond when the financial system is threatened . . . , it may be that changes in the clearing and settlement system can be safely restricted to improvements to the technology of clearing and settlement.[14]

In a footnote, he added, "The commitment of the government to provide ex post insurance also gives some basis for government interest in, and regulation of, the clearing and settlement system. Government oversight of many aspects of the financial system is of course already a fact of life."[15] Title VIII fulfills the vision Bernanke set out two decades ago. It offers a formal mechanism by which the government can "provide ex post insurance" to clearinghouses, but, in exchange, heightens the government's regulatory authority over those entities.[16]

Title VIII, through its broad and ambiguously worded delegations of authority, has given regulators a blank check to seek out companies they want to regulate as systemic or potentially systemic. The title is yet another instance in which Dodd-Frank's drafters decided that regulators, armed with a lot of discretion about whom to regulate and how, will be able to prevent another financial crisis. The drafters also gave the regulators the emergency option to open the discount window during times of crisis to an additional set of entities. Given the regulatory push toward clearing, Title VIII helps the marketplace build into its expectations the moral-hazard-inducing belief that clearinghouses are entities the government would not permit to fail.

NOTES

1. *Dodd-Frank Wall Street Reform and Consumer Protection Act,* § 804(a). The "likely to become" language makes the concept of systemic importance even more open-ended than it would otherwise be.
2. Ibid., § 803(9).
3. Ibid., § 805(a)(1).
4. Ibid., § 805(a)(2). The Fed can appeal to the FSOC if the SEC or CFTC has failed to adopt adequate standards.
5. Service providers to designated financial market utilities are also subject to examination. Ibid., § 807(b).
6. The FSOC also has the authority to require any financial institution (which is broadly defined in Ibid., § 803(5), to include any company engaged in any activity that is financial in nature or incidental thereto) to submit information to determine if its payment, clearing, or settlement activity is systemically important. Ibid., § 809(a)(2).
7. Treasury Secretary Timothy Geithner, who chairs the FSOC, recently suggested that Title VIII could be used to regulate money market funds. See Letter from

Timothy F. Geithner to members of the FSOC, September 27, 2012, http://www
.treasury.gov/connect/blog/Documents/Sec.Geithner.Letter.To.FSOC.pdf.
Geithner takes the position that the FSOC's "authority to designate systemically
important payment, clearing, or settlement activities under Title VIII of the Dodd-
Frank Act could enable the application of heightened risk-management standards
on an industry-wide basis."

8. See, for example, Andre E. Owens, Bruce H. Newman, and Elizabeth K. Derbes,
"Dodd-Frank Title VIII: The Devil Is in the Details," *WilmerHale*, September 7, 2010,
http://www.wilmerhale.com/publications/whPubsDetail.aspx?publication=9595.
The authors explain that "hidden in plain view, is a massive and expansive grant
of new authority over activities that are critically important to a broad swath of
financial institutions" and include in Appendix A an illustration of the process for
and effects of determining an activity to be systemically important.

9. *Dodd-Frank Wall Street Reform and Consumer Protection Act*, § 803(5). The scope
of activities that are financial in nature or incidental thereto is as broad as the
Fed defines it under the *Bank Holding Company Act, U.S. Code* 12 (1956), § 1843(k).
There is no de minimis threshold below which a company is beyond the reach of
the FSOC.

10. *Dodd-Frank Wall Street Reform and Consumer Protection Act*, § 805(e).

11. FSOC, "Financial Stability Oversight Council Makes First Designations in Effort
to Protect against Future Financial Crises," news release, July 18, 2012, http://
www.treasury.gov/press-center/press-releases/Pages/tg1645.aspx. FSOC voted
"to designate eight financial market utilities (FMUs) as systemically important
under Title VIII." See also FSOC, Appendix A, in 2012 *Annual Report* (Washington,
DC: FSOC, 2012), http://www.treasury.gov/initiatives/fsoc/Documents/2012%20
Appendix%20A%20Designation%20of%20Systemically%20Important%20Mar
ket%20Utilities.pdf. The appendix identifies designated entities and explains the
rationale for designating them.

12. *Dodd-Frank Wall Street Reform and Consumer Protection Act*, § 806.

13. Ibid., § 805(a)(2). The Fed is precluded, however, from involvement in decisions
with respect which types of derivatives must be cleared. Ibid., § 805(d). This is an
important limitation, because these decisions will affect clearinghouse risk.

14. Ben S. Bernanke, "Clearing and Settlement during the Crash," *The Review of
Financial Studies* 3, no. 1: 133, 150 (1990), http://www.bu.edu/econ/files/2012/01
/Bernanke-RFS.pdf.

15. Ibid., note 11.

16. In a recent speech, Bernanke continued the theme of the combination of a government backstop for clearinghouses and regulation to compensate for the moral-
hazard issues:

As is well understood, the existence of emergency credit facilities for financial market utilities could give rise to moral hazard (for example, in the form of insufficient attention by clearinghouses to establishment of private-sector liquidity arrangements in advance of a crisis). To minimize moral hazard concerns, the Federal Reserve believes it essential that the regulatory regime for these institutions include strong prudential requirements for credit and liquidity risk management, robust liquidity buffers, the maintenance of adequate amounts of high-quality collateral, and effective member-default procedures.

Bernanke, "Clearinghouses, Financial Stability, and Financial Reform," 5.

What Title IX does:

Title IX creates new offices within the SEC such as the Office of the Whistleblower, the Office of the Investor Advocate, the Office of Credit Ratings, and the Office of Municipal Securities.

It grants new enforcement powers to the SEC.

It imposes new corporate governance and executive-compensation mandates on companies.

It revises the regulation of credit rating agencies, including adding greater transparency, removing regulatory references to credit ratings, entrenching the SEC's "seal of approval" on credit ratings, and increasing legal liability of credit rating agencies.

It revises regulation of asset-backed securities, including adding a new skin-in-the-game requirement for asset securitizers.

Why Title IX's approach is flawed:

Title IX makes a laundry list of regulatory changes, most of which have nothing to do with averting financial crises.

New corporate governance and executive-compensation requirements impose unwarranted costs on companies that had nothing to do with the crisis, without offsetting benefits for investors.

The SEC's new role in assessing the accuracy of credit ratings will foster greater reliance on credit ratings, even though excessive reliance was one of the causes of the crisis.

It disproportionately burdens small credit rating agencies.

The municipal advisor category is so ambiguous that it could inadvertently draw in people who should not be covered.

The new whistleblower program could undermine internal compliance programs and reward individuals who took part in the securities violations at issue.

New enforcement powers and the manner in which the SEC uses them raise due-process concerns.

The new Office of Investor Advocate could play a large role in SEC policy, which may not help investors.

TITLE IX
Securities and Exchange Commission

T ITLE IX DEALS with a lengthy array of topics that relate primarily to the SEC, but many of them do not respond to issues that arose during the financial crisis. Title IX contains provisions regarding, among other topics, the SEC's regulation of retail financial service providers, SEC enforcement, credit rating agencies, securitization, executive compensation, internal SEC management, corporate governance, municipal securities, the Public Company Accounting Oversight Board, and SEC funding. The SEC had been asking for many of the items in Title IX before the crisis. Other items satisfied outstanding interest-group demands. Accordingly, despite ex-post attempts to draw a tenuous link, many of the provisions in Title IX bear no relationship to the crisis.[1] Other crisis-related provisions threaten to create a set of new problems. This commentary focuses on several of Title IX's ten subtitles.[2]

Subtitle A includes several measures purportedly designed to increase investor protection. First, it adds several new investor-advocacy bureaucracies at the SEC: an Office of Investor Advocate,[3] an Investor Advisory Committee,[4] and an ombudsman whose job is to resolve issues that retail investors have with the SEC or self-regulatory organizations.[5] Because one of the SEC's core missions is investor protection and the SEC already had an Office of Investor

Education and Advocacy, the need for these new entities is unclear. The head of the new Office of the Investor Advocate, appointed by the SEC chairman, could play a substantial role given the open-ended hiring authority[6] and broad mandate to make recommendations for rule changes to which the SEC must formally respond.[7] The investor advocate, who—as of November 1, 2012—has yet to be appointed, could become a powerful force within the SEC with little oversight by the SEC's politically accountable commissioners.[8] Depending on the objectives the investor advocate chooses to pursue, the new office could end up harming the investors it is supposed to help.

One of the most controversial provisions of Title IX required the SEC to study "the effectiveness of existing legal or regulatory standards of care for brokers, dealers, investment advisers," and other related persons.[9] The study responded to concerns about financial professionals' standard of care when dealing with retail customers that long predated the crisis. The fiduciary duty to which investment advisers are held is believed by many to be the duty to which brokers should be held in their dealings with retail clients. The SEC staff completed its study and made a number of recommendations, including the establishment of "a uniform fiduciary standard" and "harmonization of the broker-dealer and investment adviser regulatory regimes."[10] As SEC commissioners Paredes and Kathleen L. Casey explained, "the Study's pervasive shortcoming is that it fails to adequately justify its recommendation that the Commission embark on fundamentally changing the regulatory regime for broker-dealers and investment advisers providing personalized investment advice to retail investors."[11] Although Dodd-Frank authorized the SEC to follow the study with rulemaking,[12] the SEC has not proposed to implement the staff's recommendations.

Subtitle B of Title IX grants the SEC increased enforcement authority. For example, Dodd-Frank granted the SEC's desired authority to impose civil monetary penalties in connection with administrative settlements.[13] It already had the authority to obtain penalties through a court-approved settlement, but the new authority gives the SEC the ability to reach a settlement that includes penalties without a judicial check. Dodd-Frank also expanded the SEC's ability to bring aiding and abetting charges and enables the SEC to pursue aiding and abetting violations that were engaged in recklessly (rather than the previous "knowingly" standard).[14] The SEC has tried, although not always successfully, to use some of its new enforcement powers retroactively.[15]

Subtitle B also created a new whistleblower regime at the SEC. Massive fraud cases, like Madoff and Stanford, both of which were brought to the attention of authorities by whistleblowers, were the driving force behind the creation of the SEC's whistleblower regime and a companion CFTC regime. For any enforcement action generating monetary sanctions of more than $1 million, if the SEC determines that the whistleblower provided a qualifying tip, it does not have discretion about whether to pay an award, but rather has discretion only about how much to reward. The SEC's discretion is limited in this regard also: the award must fall within a range of 10 to 30 percent of the amount collected.[16] Even a person who is the subject of an SEC enforcement action for her role in a fraud is entitled to a whistleblower reward if she provided the relevant tip to the SEC.[17] An employee who shows that his company has discriminated against him in any manner for whistleblowing is entitled, among other things, to double back pay and compensation for attorneys' fees.[18] The whistleblower provision will likely produce some valuable information to the SEC, but the SEC is also likely to have to spend substantial resources sorting through meaningless tips and managing claims for compensation.

Subtitle C of Title IX relates to credit rating agencies, which, when registered with the SEC, are known as nationally recognized statistical rating organizations (NRSROs). The subtitle created a new SEC office for overseeing NRSROs in response to the market's ill-placed and widespread overreliance on the opinions of the three largest credit rating agencies in the years leading up to the financial crisis.[19] Regulations and private investment guidelines encouraged market participants to chase high ratings almost to the exclusion of any other considerations in selecting investments. Regulators find credit ratings to be convenient benchmarks for use in, for example, bank-capital requirements and money market fund regulations. Many market participants also use credit ratings as a substitute for due diligence.

In an effort to decrease regulatory and market reliance on ratings, Dodd-Frank required the removal of credit ratings from statutes and regulations. Rather than simply removing credit ratings, however, Dodd-Frank allows for their replacement with other "standards of credit-worthiness."[20] These new standards could become as entrenched as credit ratings were prior to the crisis. Moreover, the rest of Dodd-Frank's credit rating agency reforms threaten to undermine the positive effects of the removal of credit ratings from statutes and regulations.

First, Dodd-Frank, in the guise of being tough on credit rating agencies, solidifies the competitive advantage of the largest credit rating agencies and threatens the existence of their smaller rivals. Dodd-Frank's new requirements for credit rating agencies are designed with the biggest rating agencies in mind and are inconsistent with more specialized, smaller rating agencies.[21] These smaller rating agencies tend to have deep expertise about certain market sectors and may be paid by users of their ratings rather than by the issuers of the product being rated. Requirements related to the organizational structure and governance of credit rating agencies are disproportionately burdensome for smaller credit rating agencies. It is not clear whether the SEC will use its exemptive authority to provide meaningful exemptions for smaller rating agencies, but some small

NRSROs have already responded to the regulatory burdens by giving up their NRSRO status or declining to expand.[22] Section 933 of Dodd-Frank makes it easier to sue credit rating agencies, even those that are not registered as NRSROs. Large rating agencies have top-quality legal resources devoted to fending off such actions, but their smaller rivals are less able to defend themselves from legal attacks. The increased legal exposure could lead rating agencies to issue lower ratings than they otherwise would in order to lower their chances of being sued.[23]

Second, by explicitly directing the SEC to assess the quality of ratings, Dodd-Frank entrenches the view that NRSROs' work has a government imprimatur. Title IX empowers the SEC to suspend or revoke an NRSRO's authority to rate a particular class of securities if the SEC determines that it has failed to produce accurate ratings.[24] SEC examiners, who are not using the ratings, are not as well equipped to assess the quality of the service provided by the rating agencies as the investors who rely on ratings to make invest-ment decisions. Moreover, it is a marked departure from the SEC's traditional role as a disclosure facilitator, rather than an investment adviser. The SEC will be further entrenched in the ratings process if, as Dodd-Frank authorizes it to do, it establishes a system for assign-ing the responsibility for rating new structured finance products. A system in which a governmental or quasi-governmental entity doles out work to different credit rating agencies would likely lower the quality of NRSROs and increase the public perception that the SEC approves their work.

Subtitle D relates to asset-backed securities, which were cen-tral to the crisis. Nevertheless, the key component of the subtitle is risk retention, which is best described as a legislative response to a catchy slogan, "skin in the game," that caught on during the Dodd-Frank drafting process.[25] Section 941 imposes a one-size-fits-all 5 percent credit risk retention requirement on securitizers of asset-backed securities, except for those subject to an exemption. A key exemption is the qualified residential mortgage (QRM) exemption. Dodd-Frank charged a joint group of regulators with implementing risk retention and setting the parameters for QRMs. They issued a proposal,[26] but their efforts have stalled. The scope of QRM,[27] the exemption that the regulators gave to Fannie Mae and Freddie Mac as long as they are in government conservatorship, and the "premium capture cash reserve account" are among the most controversial aspects of the regulators' proposal. The risk-retention requirements, which could profoundly influence the manner in which the postcrisis mortgage markets develop, have been an unfortunate distraction for regulators and market participants from the more meaningful changes Dodd-Frank made to improve disclosure about the assets underlying asset-backed securities.[28]

Subtitles E and G relate to executive compensation and corporate governance. Many of these provisions fulfill objectives that interest groups had been attempting prior to the crisis to achieve by lobbying the SEC. For example, Title IX mandates shareholder say-on-pay votes at public companies,[29] requires public companies to disclose the ratio of the median employee's pay to the CEO's pay,[30] and authorizes the SEC to promulgate proxy access rules.[31] The SEC moved quickly after Dodd-Frank to adopt a rule with respect to the latter provision, but the rule was overturned in a legal challenge.[32] Title IX's corporate governance and executive-compensation provisions are, in the eyes of one expert on such matters, examples of "quack corporate governance."[33] These provisions are, at a minimum, a distraction from the more pressing postcrisis work on the SEC's agenda.

Subtitle H, which creates a new Office of Municipal Securities and makes related changes with respect to the municipal securities market, was not a response to the crisis. Although there had been long-standing concerns about the municipal securities markets, the manner in which the solutions were drafted and are now being implemented raises a host of new issues. One of the key elements of the municipal securities changes is a new regulatory regime for municipal advisors, a response to concerns that municipalities had gotten into trouble because of the poor financial advice they had received. Among the components of that regime are registration requirements,[34] professional standards set by the Municipal Securities Rulemaking Board (MSRB),[35] and a fiduciary duty to the municipalities to which municipal advisors provide advice with respect to municipal financial products or municipal securities.[36] The registration requirement went into effect October 1, 2010, but the SEC has yet to finalize its definition of who constitutes a municipal advisor. Instead, the SEC adopted (and has subsequently extended) an interim final temporary rule and proposed a permanent rule.[37] In reliance upon the statute's vague language, the SEC has interpreted the term "municipal advisor" very broadly. The term is potentially broad enough to include, for example, bank employees providing routine banking services to municipalities, volunteer appointed board members of local government units, university governing board members, board members of certain nonprofit organizations, and associations representing municipalities. The ambiguity of the reach of the new municipal advisor regime, the fact that it affects so many people who are not normally within the sights of the SEC and MSRB, and the SEC's delay in taking final action makes this a portion of Dodd-Frank fraught with potential unintended consequences.

Title IX's municipal securities provisions give rise to a number of other problems. Dodd-Frank changed the governance structure and mission of the MSRB, the self-regulatory organization that oversees the municipal markets. The new mission awkwardly requires the MSRB to protect municipal entities, along with investors. Municipal entities are the issuers of municipal securities, so their interests may be at odds with the interests of investors in municipal securities.[38] As another example, Dodd-Frank requires that when fines are imposed for violations of the MSRB's rules, they are shared between the MSRB and the entity that brings the enforcement action.[39] Allowing regulators to supplement their budgets with fine revenue undermines regulators' objectivity in writing rules and determining when to bring actions and what types of penalties to impose.

Title IX, which accounts for many of Dodd-Frank's pages, addresses a variety of topics largely unrelated to one another or to the financial crisis. Its many mandates and new bureaucracies charged with implementing those mandates may end up harming the securities markets and investors.

NOTES

1. Many of these provisions require the SEC to conduct studies on a wide array of topics, from financial literacy to extraterritorial private rights of action. While not rulemaking mandates, these study requirements—many of which had to be completed quickly—absorbed considerable staff time and served as a distraction from the SEC's many rulemaking obligations under Dodd-Frank.
2. This discussion is illustrative and by no means exhaustive. Title IX is long and includes many provisions not covered in this commentary but that are, nevertheless, significant and problematic.
3. *Dodd-Frank Wall Street Reform and Consumer Protection Act*, § 915.
4. Ibid., § 911.
5. Ibid., § 919D.
6. See *Securities Exchange Act*, § 4(g)(3), which provides that after consulting with the chairman, the investor advocate "may retain or employ independent counsel, research staff, and service staff as the Investor Advocate deems necessary to carry out the functions, powers, and duties of the Office."
7. Ibid., § 4(g)(3).
8. The SEC chairman is required to consult with, but not to obtain the assent of, the other commissioners in appointing the investor advocate. Ibid., § 4(g)(2)(A)(ii). In this regard, the investor advocate will not be unlike other senior staff at the SEC. Nevertheless, because the investor advocate has direct reporting authority to Congress, has the power to make recommendations to which the commission *must* respond, and has the ability to hire as many staff as he wants, the investor advocate

will be more powerful than other senior staff at the SEC. Ibid., § 4(g).

9. *Dodd-Frank Wall Street Reform and Consumer Protection Act,* § 913(b).

10. SEC, *Study on Investment Advisers and Broker-Dealers: As Required by Section 913 of the Dodd-Frank Wall Street Reform and Consumer Protection Act,* 112th Cong., 1st sess. (Washington, DC, January 2011), http://www.sec.gov/news /studies/2011/913studyfinal.pdf.

11. Kathleen L. Casey and Troy A. Paredes, "Statement Regarding Study on Investment Advisers and Broker-Dealers" (speech, SEC, Washington, DC, January 21, 2011), http://www.sec.gov/news/speech/2011/spch012211klctap.htm.

12. *Dodd-Frank Wall Street Reform and Consumer Protection Act,* § 913(g).

13. Ibid., § 929P.

14. Ibid., §§ 929M and 929O.

15. See, for example, *SEC v. Daifotis,* 2011 WL 2183314, Fed. Sec. L. Rep. 96,325 (N.D. Cal. June 6, 2011). The court rejects the SEC's attempt to use authority under Dodd-Frank § 929M(2)(b) retroactively. For a thoughtful discussion of retroactivity and Dodd-Frank, see Kathleen L. Casey, "Address to Practicing Law Institute's *SEC Speaks in 2011* Program" (speech, SEC, Washington, DC, February 4, 2011), http:// www.sec.gov/news/speech/2011/spch020411klc.htm.

16. *Dodd-Frank Wall Street Reform and Consumer Protection Act,* § 922, which adds 15 U.S.C. § 78u-6(b).

17. The statute does preclude recovery by, for example, employees of regulatory agencies. Interestingly, there is no statutory prohibition on the receipt of whistleblower awards by members of Congress and their staff based on information gained in the course of their official duties.

18. *Dodd-Frank Wall Street Reform and Consumer Protection Act,* § 922, which adds 15 U.S.C. § 78u-6(h).

19. See, for example, Frank Partnoy, "Overdependence on Credit Ratings Was a Primary Cause of the Crisis" (paper presented at the Eleventh Annual International Banking Conference, Federal Reserve Bank of Chicago, and the European Central Bank, Credit Market Turmoil of 2007–08: Implications for Public Policy, September 25, 2008), 1, http://www.law.yale.edu/documents/pdf/cbl/Partnoy_Overde pendence_Credit.pdf. Partnoy notes that regulators' and market participants' overdependence on credit ratings was an important cause of the crisis.

20. *Dodd-Frank Wall Street Reform and Consumer Protection Act,* §§ 939 and 939A.

21. As of the end of 2010, the three largest NRSROs, Standard & Poor's, Moody's, and Fitch, respectively had 1.2 million, 1 million, and 505,000 ratings outstanding. The next biggest rating agency, DBRS, had 42,000 ratings outstanding. SEC, *2011 Summary Report of Commission Staff's Examination of Each Nationally Recognized Statistical Rating Organization: As Required by Section 15E(p)(3)(C) of the Securities Exchange Act of 1934,* 112th Cong., 1st sess. (September 2011), 6, 19, http://www.sec

.gov/news/studies/2011/2011_nrsro_section15e_examinations_summary_report .pdf. The SEC staff found that four of the smaller credit rating agencies were not devoting sufficient staff resources to compliance because, for example, the designated compliance officer was not devoted entirely to compliance. In a relatively small organization, it is not surprising that there would not be one employee dedicated entirely to compliance.

22. One small NRSRO, which fought for years to gain this status, filed its withdrawal papers. R&I, "R&I to Withdraw from NRSRO Registration with the USSEC," news release, October 14, 2011). A.M. Best, another of the smaller NRSROs, explained that "burdensome costs were a contributing factor in A.M. Best's recent decision to discontinue its expansion into bank and hospital ratings." Comment letter from Larry G. Mayewski to Elizabeth M. Murphy, August 8, 2011, 9, http://www .sec.gov/comments/s7-18-11/s71811-39.pdf. The SEC recently brought an enforcement action against another of the small rating agencies. "In the Matter of Egan-Jones Ratings and Sean Egan, Order Instituting Administrative Cease-and-Desist Proceedings Pursuant to Sections 15E(d) and 21C of the Securities Exchange Act of 1934," Release No. 66854, April 24, 2012, http://www.sec.gov/litigation/ad min/2012/34-66854.pdf. In response, Egan-Jones, alleging an SEC bias in favor of larger, issuer-paid credit rating agencies, sued to move the matter to federal court. *Egan-Jones v. SEC,* case no. 1:12-cv-00920 (D.D.C June 6, 2012).

23. For this point, the author credits an anonymous reviewer.

24. *Dodd-Frank Wall Street Reform and Consumer Protection Act,* § 932.

25. For a discussion of some of the problems with the risk-retention requirement, see House Committee on Oversight and Regulatory Reform, Subcommittee on TARP, Financial Services, and Bailouts of Public and Private Programs, *Transparency as an Alternative to the Federal Government's Regulation of Risk Retention,* 112th Cong., 1st sess. (May 11, 2011) (statement of Anthony B. Sanders), http://mercatus .org/publication/transparency-alternative-federal-governments-regulation-risk -retention.

26. OCC et al., "Credit Risk Retention," Notice of Proposed Rulemaking, F*ederal Register* 76 (April 29, 2011), 24090.

27. Many, including once-zealous advocates of the skin-in-the-game requirement, are urging regulators to make the QRM exemption broader than proposed. Among other criteria, as proposed, a QRM would be required to have a 20 percent down payment.

28. See, for example, *Dodd-Frank Wall Street Reform and Consumer Protection Act,* § 942(b), which adds *U.S. Code* 15, § 77g(c) to require increased disclosure about the assets backing asset-backed securities.

29. Ibid., § 951.

30. Ibid., § 953(b). This provision is likely to be extremely burdensome for companies

to calculate and is of questionable relevance to investors.

31. Ibid., § 971.

32. *Business Roundtable v. SEC*, 647 F.3d 1144 (D.C. Cir. 2011). For an assessment of the effect of the proxy access rule on company value, see Thomas Stratmann and J. W. Verret, "Does Shareholder Proxy Access Damage Share Value in Small Publicly Traded Companies?" *Stanford Law Review* 64 (2012): 1431.

33. Stephen M. Bainbridge, "Dodd-Frank: Quack Federal Corporate Governance Round II," *Minnesota Law Review* 95 (2011): 1779. Bainbridge assesses the provisions in Title IX related to say-on-pay, compensation committees, executive compensation disclosures, clawbacks, proxy access, and chairman/chief executive officer disclosure.

34. *Dodd-Frank Wall Street Reform and Consumer Protection Act*, § 975(a)(1)(B).

35. Ibid., § 975(b)(2)(L), which adds *U.S. Code* 15 § 78o-4(b)(2)(L).

36. Ibid., § 975(c), which adds *U.S. Code* 15 § 78o-4(c)(2).

37. Rule 15Ba2-6T [17 CFR 240.15Ba2-6T]. The SEC most recently extended the interim final temporary rule on September 21, 2012. SEC, "Extension of Temporary Registration of Municipal Advisors," Release No. 34-67901. The SEC has proposed, but not adopted, a permanent rule. SEC, "Registration of Municipal Advisors," Notice of Proposed Rulemaking, *Federal Register* 76 (January 6, 2011), 824. See also Thomas K. Potter and Benjamin B. Coulter, "Hurry Up and Wait: Municipal Advisor Registration," *Thomson Reuters News & Insight*, April 19, 2012. Potter and Coulter describe the chronology and difficulties associated with rulemaking under Dodd-Frank related to municipal advisor registration.

38. For example, investors may want municipal entities to disclose matters related to their pension obligations that municipal entities would prefer not to disclose. See, for example, Eileen Norcross, "Getting an Accurate Picture of State Pension Liabilities," *Mercatus on Policy*, No. 85 (Arlington, VA: Mercatus Center at George Mason University, December 2010), http://mercatus.org/sites/default/files/pub lication/Getting%20an%20Accurate%20Picture%20of%20State%20Pension%20 Liablilities.Norcross.12.13.10_1.pdf.

39. *Dodd-Frank Wall Street Reform and Consumer Protection Act*, § 975(c)(8), which adds *U.S. Code* 15, § 78o-4(c)(9). The MSRB does not have authority to enforce its own rules but relies on regulatory authorities, including the SEC and FINRA, to do so.

What Title X does:

Title X creates the Consumer Financial Protection Bureau (CFPB).

It transfers consumer financial protection responsibilities to the CFPB.

It gives the CFPB broad new regulatory powers.

It includes the Durbin amendment, which directs the Fed to cap the fees banks can charge merchants for debit card transactions.

Why Title X's approach is flawed:

CFPB's structure eliminates accountability to the American people. It is an autonomous agency located within the Fed but without oversight from the Fed or Congress, without a bipartisan commission structure, without a safety and soundness mandate, and with a large budget with no strings attached.

The CFPB's authority is written broadly and is being interpreted even more broadly. As a result, the range of consumer financial products is likely to be limited, and consumers will likely pay more for the products to which they have access.

The Durbin amendment imposes market-distorting price controls. It may benefit retailers, but it will likely result in increased bank fees for consumers.

TITLE X
Consumer Financial Protection Bureau

T ITLE X, WHICH creates the Bureau of Consumer Financial Protection (CFPB), is one of the centerpieces of Dodd-Frank.[1] The CFPB is remarkable for its peculiar structure and its lack of oversight and accountability. Its authority is far reaching, ambiguously defined, and unbalanced. Its unprecedented structure will impede its mission of protecting consumers.[2]

Recently, CFPB director Richard Cordray explained the purpose of his agency:

> We are the first agency ever created with the sole purpose of protecting consumers in the financial marketplace. It is no easy task, but it is crucial because the financial marketplace is no easy place for our fellow citizens as they seek to manage their affairs. Our task is also crucial because, as we saw with the recent financial crisis, unregulated or poorly regulated financial markets can undermine the stability of the economy and with it the promotion of the general welfare that, as specified in the preamble to the Constitution, stands as one of the basic purposes of the federal government. For that reason, the new Consumer Bureau was also created to help ensure that the recent financial panic and economic meltdown does not repeat itself.[3]

The latter part of the director's explanation suggests that the CFPB will help to prevent another crisis by regulating the financial markets in a manner that fosters economic stability.

Economic stability is not one of the identified purposes of the CFPB,[4] however, nor is economic stability among the CFPB's objectives. Instead, the CFPB "is authorized to exercise its authorities under Federal consumer financial law for the purposes of" making sure consumers are informed and protected, reducing unnecessary regulatory burdens, consistently enforcing consumer financial law, and making sure the consumer financial-products markets are working.[5] The CFPB lacks the integrated mandate to consider both the effectiveness of its consumer financial protection regulations and how they will affect the safety and soundness of the entities it regulates.

Absent such an integrated view, the CFPB could contribute to the next crisis by destabilizing its regulated entities through the imposition of imprudent regulations. As Bernanke explains, separating consumer protection from the rest of banking regulation comes at a cost:

> Both the substance of consumer protection rules and their enforcement are complementary to prudential supervision. Poorly designed financial products and misaligned incentives can at once harm consumers and undermine financial institutions. Indeed, as with subprime mortgages and securities backed by these mortgages, these products may at times also be connected to systemic risk. At the same time, a determination of how to regulate financial practices both effectively and efficiently can be facilitated by the understanding of institutions' practices and systems that is gained through safety and soundness regulation and supervision. Similarly, risk assessment and compliance monitoring of consumer and

prudential regulations are closely related, and thus entail both informational advantages and resource savings.[6]

Other agencies cannot force the CFPB to take safety and soundness into account. Directives for the CFPB to consult with other regulators "concerning the consistency of the proposed rule with prudential, market, or systemic objectives administered by such agencies" do not alter CFPB's mission, which does not include any of these objectives.[7] Moreover, while the FSOC can overturn a CFPB rule, it can do so only on the timely written petition of another FSOC member and with the votes of two-thirds of the council.[8] That voting standard is a difficult hurdle, particularly because the CFPB director has one of the votes. The only basis on which a CFPB rule can be overturned is if it "would put the safety and soundness of the United States banking system or the stability of the financial system of the United States at risk."[9] The FSOC is consequently unlikely to provide much of a check on the CFPB.

The CFPB's mission is flawed not only for what it does not include, but also for what it does include. The CFPB has the power to prohibit unfair, deceptive, or abusive acts or practices.[10] The latter term is new and the statute does not provide clear parameters for it beyond explaining that an abusive act or practice must either "materially interfere with the ability of a consumer to understand a term or condition" or "take unreasonable advantage of" the consumer's "lack of understanding" or "inability of the consumer to protect the interests of the consumer."[11] As Professor Todd Zywicki has explained, the abusive standard "appears to be a return to old-fashioned substantive regulation" in place of modern disclosure-based regulation.[12] Cordray has suggested that there will not be a rulemaking to define "abusive." Instead, it will be interpreted according to the facts and circumstances.[13] In other words, regulated entities will have to piece together what the term means based upon the facts and circumstances of the CFPB's and state attorneys general's enforcement actions. There will be no rulemaking process to guide them, offer them an opportunity for comment, or forewarn them to avoid certain practices.

The deficiencies in the CFPB's mission are only magnified by the deficiencies in its structure. Unlike other comparable regulators, the CFPB is not run by a bipartisan commission or board, but by a single director. The politically balanced commissions at agencies like the SEC, the CFTC, and the Federal Trade Commission help to moderate those agencies. Once appointed by the president with the advice and consent of the Senate, the CFPB's director serves for five years, and the president has only a limited ability to remove him from office.[14] (On January 4, 2012, President Obama appointed the CFPB's first director through a legally and politically controversial recess appointment, without a Senate vote.) As Zywicki explains, "As an unaccountable bureaucracy with a single head, the bureau will be susceptible to bureaucracy's worst pathologies: a tunnel-vision focus on the agency's regulatory mission, undue risk aversion and agency overreach."[15]

On paper, the agency is located within the Fed, but the Fed is powerless to affect the CFPB's actions.[16] The CFPB director determines the agency's annual budget, which is funded by Fed earnings and, starting with fiscal year 2013, can be as high as 12 percent of the Fed's operating expenses as reported in the 2009 Annual Report and adjusted for inflation, which would mean a budget of nearly half a billion dollars.[17] Congressional appropriators are specifically precluded from reviewing the CFPB's use of funds from the Fed.

The CFPB's broad mission and lack of accountability could harm consumers. As Zywicki explains,

The new consumer credit "super regulator" could prove an economy killer, producing still-higher credit costs for consumers, and accelerating regulatory pressures that drive consumers out of the mainstream financial system and into the alternative, high-cost financial sector. Moreover, because millions of small, independent businesses rely wholly or partly on personal and consumer credit to start and build their businesses, heavy-handed, misguided regulation could strangle job creation and economic dynamism.[18]

These costs may be difficult to see, particularly if the CFPB does not make a commitment to carry out thorough regulatory analysis prior to adopting rules. The CFPB is subject to limited economic analysis requirements, but the analysis the CFPB conducts is exempt from review by the president's Office of Information and Regulatory Affairs.[19]

Another provision of Title X that was supposed to benefit consumers but actually may end up hurting them is the so-called Durbin amendment.[20] The result of a long power struggle between large retailers and banks that issue debit cards, the Durbin amendment directed the Fed to cap the fees banks can charge merchants for debit card transactions. In the process, it harms consumers. Price controls do not tend to benefit consumers, and the price controls on interchange fees are likely to be no different.[21] Consumers may pay higher fees to banks and not enjoy offsetting savings from retailers. In April 2012, credit rating agency Standard & Poor's commented:

> Consistent with our original expectations, the implementation of the Durbin Amendment has had no immediate impact on U.S. bank ratings. Banks have responded to the lost swipe fee revenue by introducing new bank service and product fees. Furthermore, there is little direct evidence that merchants have passed on the savings from lower interchange fees to their customers, suggesting that the legislation may be falling short on its goals for consumers.[22]

Title X is cited by proponents of Dodd-Frank as one of its corner-stones. In constructing the new CFPB, Congress delegated enormous power over a large portion of our economy to a single person who is not accountable to Congress, the president, or the public. The CFPB may use these powers in a way that neither helps the consumers Title X intended to protect nor enhances the nation's financial stability.

NOTES

1. The statute refers to the new agency as "the Bureau of Consumer Financial Protection," but the agency is commonly referred to as "the Consumer Financial Protection Bureau," which is the basis for the acronym.

2. For a thorough analysis of the agency in its historical framework, see Todd J. Zywicki, "The Consumer Financial Protection Bureau: Savior or Menace?" (working paper 12-25, Mercatus Center at George Mason University, Arlington, VA, October 2012), http://mercatus.org/sites/default/files/CFPB_Zywicki_v1-0_1.pdf.

3. Richard Cordray, "Prepared Remarks" (speech, American Constitution Society Conference, Washington, DC, June 15, 2012), http://www.consumerfinance.gov /speeches/prepared-remarks-by-richard-cordray-at-the-american-constitution -society-conference.

4. *Dodd-Frank Wall Street Reform and Consumer Protection Act,* § 1021(a).

5. Ibid., § 1021(b).

6. House Committee on Financial Services, *Regulatory Restructuring,* 111th Cong., 1st sess. (July 24, 2009) (statement of Ben S. Bernanke), http://www.federalreserve .gov/newsevents/testimony/bernanke20090724a.htm.

7. *Dodd-Frank Wall Street Reform and Consumer Protection Act,* § 1031(e).

8. Ibid., § 1023.

9. Ibid., § 1023(a).

10. Ibid., § 1031.

11. Ibid., § 1031(d).

12. Zywicki, "The Consumer Financial Protection Bureau: Savior or Menace?," 67.

13. House Financial Services Committee, 112th Cong., 2d sess. (Mar. 29, 2012) (statement of Richard Cordray), http://www.consumerfinance.gov/speeches/testimony -of-richard-cordray-before-the-u-s-house-of-representatives. In response to a question from committee chairman Spencer Bachus, Cordray stated that the term "abusive" would be interpreted "on a facts and circumstances basis," rather than

defined by rule.

14. *Dodd-Frank Wall Street Reform and Consumer Protection Act,* § 1011.

15. House Committee on Oversight and Government Relations, Subcommittee on TARP, Financial Services, and Bailouts of Public and Private Programs, *Who's Watching the Watchmen? Oversight of the Consumer Financial Protection Bureau,* 112th Cong., 1st sess. (May 24, 2011) (statement of Todd Zywicki), 3, http://merca tus.org/sites/default/files/Zywiki-Testimony-5.24.11.pdf.

16. *Dodd-Frank Wall Street Reform and Consumer Protection Act,* § 1012(c)(2), which grants the CFPB autonomy from the Fed.

17. Ibid., § 1017. If that turns out not to be enough, the director can ask Congress for an additional $200 million each year. Ibid., § 1017(e). In addition, the CFPB has established a Civil Penalty Fund under Dodd-Frank (§ 1017(d)) to collect the penalties it assesses in enforcement actions. Any money not paid to victims will be available to the CFPB for consumer education and financial-literacy programs. See CFPB, "Civil Penalty Fund," http://files.consumerfinance.gov/f/201207_cfpb_civil_pen alty_fund_factsheet.pdf. The CFPB fact sheet describes the organization's plans for using Civil Penalty Fund money "to hire outside contractors to conduct those programs."

18. House Subcommittee on TARP, Financial Services, and Bailouts of Public and Private Programs, *Who's Watching the Watchmen?* (Zywicki statement), 1–2.

19. *Dodd-Frank Wall Street Reform and Consumer Protection Act,* § 1022(b)(2), which requires the CFPB to consider "the potential benefits and costs to consumers and covered persons" and "the impact of proposed rules on" small banks and credit unions and rural consumers. As an independent regulatory agency, the CFPB is subject neither to the executive orders governing economic analysis nor to review by the Office of Information and Regulatory Affairs.

20. *Dodd-Frank Wall Street Reform and Consumer Protection Act,* § 1075, which amends *U.S. Code* 15, § 16930-2.

21. Todd Zywicki and Josh Wright, "Durbin's Antitrust Fantasies," *Washington Times,* June 17, 2010, http://www.washingtontimes.com/news/2010/jun/17/durbins-an titrust-fantasies/?page=1. Zywicki and Wright explain, "The result would be to shift those costs onto consumers, resulting in the end of free checking for many consumers, new fees or limits on debit card transactions and higher overdraft charges. In exchange, consumers are given a speculative promise that some undetermined part of this merchant cost reduction might get passed on to them in the form of lower retail prices." See also John Berlau, "Issue Analysis: Government Barriers to Georgia's Growth; How Dodd-Frank Price Controls Poach the Peach State's Prosperity," (Georgia Public Policy Foundation and Competitive Enterprise Institute, June 26, 2012), http://cei.org/sites/default/files/John%20Berlau%20 -%20Government%20Barriers%20to%20Georgia's%20Growth.pdf. Berlau writes,

"If banks and credit unions can't make a profit or even cover costs on what they charge retailers to process debit cards, they will have to make it up in significant part through what they charge their customers." See also Todd J. Zywicki, "The Economics of Payment Card Interchange Fees and the Limits of Regulation" (working paper, International Center for Law and Economics Regulatory Program, June 2, 2010), http://mercatus.org/sites/default/files/zywicki_interchange.pdf. Zywicki argues, in the context of credit card interchange fees, that government intervention can harm consumers.

22. See, for example, Standard & Poor's, "U.S. Banks Are Changing Their Strategies to Mitigate the Financial Impact of the Durbin Amendment," April 30, 2012, http://www.standardandpoors.com/ratings/articles/en/us/?articleType=HTML&assetID=1245333051340.

What Title XI does:

Title XI amends the Fed's emergency lending authority
to mandate broad-based eligibility, forbid bailing out
insolvent firms, and require Treasury sign-off.

It requires congressional approval for FDIC
emergency-guarantee programs.

It increases Fed transparency by, among other things, requiring the
Fed to make its open-market purchases of securities and discount
window activities publicly available after a two-year lag.

It directs the GAO to audit the Fed's financial-crisis assistance programs.

Why Title XI's approach is flawed:

Title XI did not mandate continuous GAO audits of the Fed.

Title XI's enhancements to Fed transparency are not sufficient given
the Fed's increased regulatory authority under Dodd-Frank.

TITLE XI

Fed Transparency and Bailouts

by James Broughel

ITLE XI IS intended to provide for greater transparency of Fed actions during crises and normal periods, to create greater accountability for Fed officials during times of crisis, and to tighten the constraints on the Fed's emergency-lending programs.

During the financial crisis of 2008, the Fed heavily utilized its long-dormant emergency lending authority under section 13(3) of the Federal Reserve Act (FRA).[1] This section of the FRA enables the Fed to create special lending programs during "unusual and exigent circumstances." In hopes of easing the crisis, the Fed used its section 13(3) power to create a number of emergency-lending programs. The Fed drew criticism in connection with some of these programs, particularly those aimed at rescuing individual institutions. Table 1 displays programs instituted during this period.

Dodd-Frank made several changes to the Fed's emergency authorities under section 13(3). The Fed, in consultation with the Treasury secretary, must write procedures for how its emergency-lending programs will operate. Under the revised section 13(3), these programs must have "broad-based eligibility"[2] and must be designed to provide

Table 1. Special Federal Reserve Emergency-Lending Facilities, December 2007–July 2010

Name of Program	Description
Term Auction Facility	Auctioned one-month and three-month discount window loans to eligible depository institutions
Dollar Swap Lines	Opened dollar swap lines to foreign central banks
Term Securities Lending Facility	Auctioned loans of US Treasury securities to primary dealers against eligible collateral
Primary Dealer Credit Facility	Allowed overnight cash loans to primary dealers against eligible collateral
Asset-Backed Commercial Paper Money Market Mutual Fund Liquidity	Made loans to depository institutions and their affiliates to finance purchases of eligible asset-backed commercial paper from money market mutual funds
Commercial Paper Funding Facility (CPFF)	Provided loans to a special purpose vehicle to finance purchases of new issues of asset-backed commercial paper and unsecured commercial paper from eligible issuers
Money Market Investor Funding Facility	Helped finance purchase of eligible short-term debt obligations held by money market mutual funds
Term Asset-Backed Securities Loan Facility (TALF)	Made loans to eligible investors to finance purchases of eligible asset-backed securities
Assistance to individual institutions (multiple programs)	A series of programs created to provide special assistance to individual firms, including Bear Stearns, AIG, Citigroup, and Bank of America.

Source: GAO, "Federal Reserve System: Opportunities Exist to Strengthen Policies and Processes for Managing Emergency Assistance" (GAO-11-696, Washington, DC, July 11, 2011), 3–4.

"liquidity to the financial system," and not to bail out failing financial institutions.[3] Taxpayer protection is emphasized by requiring that the policies "be designed to ensure . . . the security for emergency loans is sufficient to protect taxpayers from losses and that any such program is terminated in a timely and orderly fashion."[4] The Fed is also prohibited from using these programs to lend to insolvent borrowers.[5] (As we saw during the last crisis, however, the line between deep liquidity problems and solvency is not always easy to discern.) This requirement should help define the Fed's role as a lender of last resort and is in line with traditional definitions of the lender-of-last-resort function that have existed throughout history.[6]

Importantly, the changes also insert a measure of political accountability into emergency lending. The Fed is required to obtain the prior approval of the Treasury for any program under section 13(3).[7] Within a week of establishing a program, the Fed also has to provide Congress with a justification for the program, a description of its terms, and a list of recipients.[8] The Fed has to provide monthly updates, including estimates of collateral value and the costs to taxpayers.[9] Dodd-Frank also authorizes the GAO to audit emergency-lending facilities.[10] Finally, Dodd-Frank provides for delayed public transparency with respect to section13(3) lending.[11]

Dodd-Frank placed companion restrictions on the ability of the FDIC to guarantee banks during a crisis. The FDIC is authorized to "create a widely available program to guarantee obligations of solvent" banks and bank holding companies and their affiliates "during times of severe economic distress."[12] Equity injections are precluded.[13] A written determination approved by a supermajority of the FDIC and Fed that there is "a liquidity event" is a prerequisite to an FDIC guarantee program.[14] The GAO is required to review the determination.[15] The FDIC cannot issue any guarantees until Congress, upon request by the president and by joint resolution, has approved the program.[16] Like the section 13(3) changes, these constraints on the FDIC add much-needed political accountability and transparency to financial-crisis interventions.

In addition to the limits placed upon emergency interventions, Title XI of Dodd-Frank also provided new transparency into the

Fed's routine activities, which have traditionally been opaque. First, Dodd-Frank required that the Fed make GAO reports, its financial statements, and other information related to the Fed's "accounting, financial reporting, and internal controls" available online.[17] Second, Dodd-Frank mandated ongoing public transparency—after a two-year lag—with respect to the Fed's open-market purchases of securities and discount-window activities.[18] Finally, Dodd-Frank directed the GAO to conduct a one-time, independent audit of the Fed's emergency-lending programs during the financial crisis, an area beyond the purview of regular financial statement audits.[19]

The new ongoing disclosure requirements push back against the Fed's historical resistance to disclosing details about its transactions with financial institutions. The Fed's secretive tendencies manifested themselves most dramatically in connection with its reluctance to provide information with respect to AIG's counterparties during the crisis[20] and its recent Freedom of Information Act (FOIA) dispute with Bloomberg and Fox News. Although discount window lending was exempted from the GAO audit, Bloomberg and Fox News placed a FOIA request for detailed disclosure of crisis-period discount window transactions and other Fed transactions. After the Fed resisted all the way to the Supreme Court, Bloomberg and Fox News prevailed and the information was released to them in March 2011.[21] Bloomberg later made the data available to the public in December 2011.[22]

Some scholars have echoed the Fed's concerns about transparency. Milton Friedman and Anna Schwartz made a similar argument when discussing the Reconstruction Finance Corporation (RFC), a Depression-era provider of loans to banks, other financial institutions, and railroads:

An act passed in July of 1932 was interpreted as requiring publication of the names of banks to which the RFC had made loans in the preceding month, and such publication began in

August. The inclusion of a bank's name on the list was correctly interpreted as a sign of weakness, and hence frequently led to bank runs on the bank.[23]

Other scholars have made similar claims,[24] and Atlee Pomerene, chairman of the RFC, once said that publication of RFC loans "was the most damnable and vicious thing that was ever done. It counteracted all the good we had been able to do."[25] Others have suggested that revealing names of banks did discourage borrowing, but that bank runs were not the result of these actions.[26]

Recent evidence suggests that revealing this information after some time has passed may not be detrimental and may in fact be in the public interest. When information was released in response to the Bloomberg and Fox FOIA lawsuits and the GAO Dodd-Frank report, there were no major disruptions in the market. In both cases, there was a considerable lag in the disclosure. Similarly, the two-year lag for Dodd-Frank mandated disclosures likely addresses concerns that might otherwise accompany such disclosures.[27] In short, Dodd-Frank seems to have taken the prudent course in allowing for greater transparency and accountability for the Fed and financial institutions in the long run while ensuring short-run stability of the financial system.

The GAO audit conducted pursuant to Dodd-Frank was a rare chance to have a third-party look inside the activities of the Fed. The resulting report revealed the identity of the institutions that participated in the emergency programs and the amounts and the terms of their borrowings.[28] The GAO made a number of important recommendations in its audit about ways to improve Fed governance and increase transparency. Specifically, the GAO recommended that the Fed

- strengthen reserve banks' formal acquisition policies related to awarding of contracts to private vendors;

- better manage reserve banks' employee conflicts of interest, especially since the Fed has now begun taking a greater role with respect to nonbank institutions, for which the reserve banks' internal policies are more vague;
- finalize a risk-management policy with respect to vendor contracts for the Federal Reserve Bank of New York;
- strengthen reserve banks' procedures for handling high-risk borrower access to emergency programs;
- create better plans for estimating and tracking losses in connection with emergency-lending programs;
- set forth processes for documenting (to the extent not otherwise required by law) justification for use of emergency section 13(3) authority in the future and integrate resulting information into policy decision making; and
- better document guidance from the Fed to the reserve banks with respect to emergency programs.[29]

The first of these recommendations highlights one of the most revealing parts of the GAO report. The Fed awarded a large number of noncompetitive contracts during the crisis. The GAO pointed out that because the reserve banks are not subject to the Federal Acquisition Regulation, they are able to employ contracting practices that would not be acceptable for government agencies.[30] The reserve banks "awarded 103 contracts worth $659.4 million from 2008 through 2010" as part of its emergency programs.[31] Eight of the ten highest-paying contracts were awarded noncompetitively.[32] Awarding contracts noncompetitively creates opportunities for cronyism, which is very destructive.[33] Table 2 shows some of the biggest beneficiaries of these contracts.

The Fed, which has been notoriously reluctant to disclose information about its activities, would not be likely to publicize this type of information voluntarily, but it would be useful for Congress to

Table 2. Examples of Vendor Fees Awarded Noncompetitively for Contracts Related to Emergency Lending Programs, 2008–10

Vendor	Total Fees Earned 2008–10	Services Provided	Program(s)
BlackRock	$194,482,594	Investment manager, valuation services	Maiden Lane Programs, Citigroup lending commitment
Morgan Stanley	$108,400,327	Investment banking advisory services	AIG Revolving Credit Facility ("AIG RCF")
Ernst & Young	$93,152,399	Due diligence	Maiden Lane Programs, Bank of America lending commitment, AIG RCF
Pacific Investment Management Company LLC	$45,633,841	Investment manager, transaction agent, valuation services	CPFF, Bank of America lending commitment
Davis Polk & Wardwell	$34,968,622	Legal services	Maiden Lane Programs, TALF, AIG RCF
State Street Corporation	$8,809,904	Administrator, custodian	CPFF
EMC	$8,455,193	Primary services	Maiden Lane Programs
Pricewaterhouse-Coopers	$7,833,199	Valuation services	Citigroup lending commitment
Sidley Austin	$4,009,325	Legal services	TALF, AIG RCF
Cleary Gottlieb Steen & Hamilton	$2,422,169	Legal services	Maiden Lane Programs

· · · · · · · · · · ·

Table 2 (*continued*)

Vendor	Total Fees Earned 2008–10	Services Provided	Program(s)
Axiom	$1,413,821	Legal services	Maiden Lane Programs
Wells Fargo	$1,300,949	Primary services	Maiden Lane Programs
Simpson Thacher & Bartlett	$1,147,617	Legal services	Maiden Lane Programs
Kelley Drye & Warren	$1,001,123	Legal services	Maiden Lane Programs

Note: Only fees earned in excess of $1 million are shown. All contracts shown were awarded noncompetitively.
Source: GAO, "Federal Reserve System: Opportunities Exist to Strengthen Policies and Processes for Managing Emergency Assistance" (GAO-11-696, Washington, DC, July 11, 2011), 168, 174, 177, 184, 187, 191, 198, and 227.

have access to information of this sort on a regular basis.

In addition to noncompetitive contracts, the GAO audit also revealed that many of the largest beneficiaries of the Fed's programs were foreign institutions. Table 3 shows the largest foreign banks to use the emergency-lending facilities.

Information with respect to government lending to foreign institutions is likely to be of particular interest to the public.[34]

A common criticism of auditing the Fed is that it will jeopardize the Fed's independence from Congress and political influence.[35] The type of independence that undergraduate money and banking textbooks describe clearly does not exist. The close collaboration of the Fed and the Treasury and the "revolving door" between them[36] is one way in which this independence is compromised. Friedman questioned the value of the ideal of Fed independence when he asked, "Is it really tolerable in a democracy to have so much power

Table 3. Largest Foreign Banks to Use Emergency-Lending Facilities, December 1, 2007–July 21, 2010

Financial Institution	Total Loans
Barclays (UK)	$868 billion
RBS (UK)	$541 billion
Deutsche Bank AG (Germany)	$354 billion
UBS AG (Switzerland)	$287 billion
Credit Suisse Group AG (Switzerland)	$262 billion
Bank of Scotland PLC (UK)	$181 billion
BNP Paribas SA (France)	$175 billion
Dexia SA (Belgium)	$159 billion
Dresdner Bank AG (Germany)	$135 billion
Société Générale SA (France)	$124 billion

Source: GAO, "Federal Reserve System: Opportunities Exist to Strengthen Policies and Processes for Managing Emergency Assistance" (GAO-11-696, Washington, DC, July 11, 2011), 131.

concentrated in a body free from any kind of direct, effective political control?"[37] He went on to suggest—with some degree of prescience—that an independent Fed may be a "dispersal of responsibility" from the Treasury and that independent Fed officials may "almost inevitably give undue emphasis to the point of view of bankers."[38] Friedman argued that monetary responsibilities and regulatory responsibilities might be better handled if they were independent of one another to avoid obscuring accountability between these two very different functions.[39] In fact, the Fed's regulatory powers were enhanced under Dodd-Frank, rather than reduced, as Friedman proposed.

While parts of Title XI appear to be movements in the right direction—greater accountability for and controls over emergency actions, and new transparency into Fed activities—Title XI could have done more. Additional transparency is needed both at the Fed Board of Governors and in the reserve banks. The GAO audit's revelations and recommendations bolster the case for greater transparency. The Fed is much more than a monetary-policy body, and Dodd-Frank only enhanced its role as regulator. Continuous GAO audits would help shed light on the Fed's effectiveness as a regulator and on its practices, including the awarding of noncompetitive contracts. The GAO's 2011 audit and the transparency measures Dodd-Frank instituted are good first steps, but more transparency is needed.

NOTES

1. *Discount of Obligations Arising out of Actual Commercial Transactions, U.S. Code* 12, § 343.
2. *Federal Reserve Act,* § 13(3)(A). A program "that is structured to remove assets from the balance sheet of a single and specific company, or . . . [to] assist a single and specific company [to] avoid bankruptcy" is not a broad-based program. Ibid., § 13(3)(B)(iii). Consequently, under the revised section 13(3), the Fed would not be able to structure a credit facility for a single market participant, such as the one it established for AIG in September 2008.
3. Ibid., § 13(3)(B)(i).
4. Ibid.
5. Ibid., § 13(3)(B)(ii).
6. See, for example, Walter Bagehot, *Lombard Street: A Description of the Money Market* (New York: Scribner, Armstrong & Co., 1873).
7. *Federal Reserve Act,* § 13(3)(B)(iv).
8. Ibid., § 13(3)(C)(i).
9. Ibid., § 13(3)(C)(ii).
10. *Dodd-Frank Wall Street Reform and Consumer Protection Act,* § 1102.
11. Ibid., § 1103.
12. Ibid., § 1105(a).
13. Ibid.
14. Ibid. That written determination must include evidence that there is a liquidity event; that, in the absence of the program, there would be "serious adverse effects on financial stability or economic conditions in the United States"; and that the program is a necessary preventative measure. Ibid., § 1104(a)(2).

15. Ibid., § 1104(c)(2).

16. Ibid., § 1105(c) and (d).

17. Ibid., § 1103(a). The required documents are available at http://www.federal reserve.gov/newsevents/reform_audit.htm.

18. *Dodd-Frank Wall Street Reform and Consumer Protection Act,* § 1103(b). Information on the composition and size of the Fed's balance sheet is available on the Fed's website. See http://www.federalreserve.gov/monetarypolicy/bst_fedsbal ancesheet.htm. Information about discount window borrowing, which was first made available at the end of September 2012, is also available on the Fed's website. See http://www.federalreserve.gov/newsevents/reform_discount_window.htm. The Fed also will make information about the Fed's open market operations available regularly. See http://www.newyorkfed.org/markets/OMO_transaction_data .html.

19. *Dodd-Frank Wall Street Reform and Consumer Protection Act,* § 1109(a)(1). See also GAO, "Federal Reserve System: Opportunities Exist to Strengthen Policies and Processes for Managing Emergency Assistance" (GAO-11-696, Washington, DC, July 11, 2011).

20. See, for example, Senate Committee on Banking, Housing, and Urban Affairs, *American International Group: Examining What Went Wrong, Government Intervention, and Implications for Future Regulation,* 111th Cong., 1st sess. (March 5, 2009), 12–13, http://www.gpo.gov/fdsys/pkg/CHRG-111shrg51303/pdf/CHRG-111shrg51303.pdf. Responding to a request from Senator Christopher Dodd for the names of the AIG counterparties, Donald L. Kohn, vice chairman of the Fed, responded, "I would be very concerned that if we started revealing lists of names who did transactions with companies who later came under government protection, got capital, that sort of thing, that people just wouldn't want to do transactions with companies."

21. *Bloomberg, L.P. v. Board of Governors,* 601 F.3d 143 (2d Cir. 2010), cert. denied *Clearinghouse Ass'n v. Bloomberg,* 131 S. Ct. 1674 (2011); *Fox News Network, LLC v. Board of Governors,* 601 F.3d 158 (2d Cir. 2010), cert. denied, *Clearing House Ass'n. v. Fox News Network,* 131 S. Ct. 1676 (2011). See also Bob Ivry and Craig Torres, "Fed's Court-Ordered Transparency Shows Americans 'Have a Right to Know,'" Bloomberg, March 22, 2011, http://www.bloomberg.com/news/2011-03-22/fed-s-court -ordered-transparency-shows-americans-have-a-right-to-know-.html; and Bradley Keoun and Craig Torres, "Foreign Banks Tapped Fed's Secret Lifeline Most at Crisis Peak," Bloomberg, April 1, 2011, http://www.bloomberg.com/news/2011-04 -01/foreign-banks-tapped-fed-s-lifeline-most-as-bernanke-kept-borrowers -secret.html.

22. See Phil Kuntz and Bob Ivry, "Fed Once-Secret Loan Crisis Data Compiled by *Bloomberg* Released to Public," Bloomberg, December 23, 2011, http://www.bloom berg.com/news/2011-12-23/fed-s-once-secret-data-compiled-by-bloomberg-re

leased-to-public.html.

23. Milton Friedman and Anna Schwartz, *A Monetary History of the United States, 1867–1960* (Princeton, NJ: Princeton University Press, 1963), 325.

24. See, for example, Laurence Sullivan, *Prelude to Panic* (Washington, DC: Statesman Press, 1936); Leland Yeager, *International Monetary Relations* (New York: Harper and Row, 1966).

25. Quoted in James L. Butkiewicz, "The Reconstruction Finance Corporation, the Gold Standard, and the Banking Panic of 1933," *Southern Economic Journal* 66 (October 1, 1999): 271.

26. Ibid., 271–293.

27. See House Committee on Financial Services, Subcommittee on Domestic Monetary Policy and Technology, *Audit the Fed: Dodd-Frank, QE3, and Federal Reserve Transparency*, 112th Cong., 1st sess. (Oct. 4, 2011) (statement of Mark A. Calabria), http://www.cato.org/publications/congressional-testimony/audit-fed-doddfrank-qe3-federal-reserve-transparency. In his testimony, Calabria notes that by giving the Fed two years to reveal discount window lending activity, the "risk that such disclosure will dissuade financial institutions from the use of the discount window has been minimized."

28. See GAO, "Federal Reserve System: Opportunities Exist to Strengthen Policies and Processes for Managing Emergency Assistance" (GAO-11-696, Washington, DC, July 11, 2011).

29. Ibid., 143–44.

30. Ibid., 58–60.

31. Ibid., 52.

32. Ibid.

33. For a discussion of cronyism, see Matthew Mitchell, "The Pathology of Privilege: The Economic Consequences of Government Favoritism" (working paper, Mercatus Center at George Mason University, Arlington, VA, July 8, 2012), http://mercatus.org/publication/pathology-privilege-economic-consequences-government-favoritism.

34. On a related note, more information is needed with respect to the swap agreements the Fed has with foreign central banks. The Fed publishes information related to swap agreements but does not specify which foreign institutions benefit. See Fed, "Credit and Liquidity Problems and the Balance Sheet," November 30, 2011, http://www.federalreserve.gov/monetarypolicy/bst_liquidityswaps.htm; and Fed, "Open Market Transactions: Transaction Data," n.d., http://www.newyorkfed.org/markets/OMO_transaction_data.html.

35. For a defense of the Fed's independence, see Ben S. Bernanke, "Central Bank Independence, Transparency, and Accountability" (speech, Institute for Monetary and Economic Studies International Conference, Bank of Japan, Tokyo, Japan, May 25,

2010), http://www.federalreserve.gov/newsevents/speech/bernanke20100525a
.htm. Bernanke acknowledged the need for "further clarify[ing] the dividing line
between monetary and fiscal responsibilities," but placed discount window lending and lender-of-last-resort functions on the monetary policy side of the line.

36. See House Subcommittee on Domestic Monetary Policy and Technology, *Audit the
Fed* (Calabria statement).

37. Milton Friedman, "Should There Be an Independent Monetary Authority?" in *In
Search of a Monetary Constitution,* ed. L. B. Yeager (Cambridge, MA: Harvard University Press, 1962), 219.

38. Ibid.

39. Milton Friedman, "Monetary Policy for the 1980s," in *To Promote Prosperity: U.S.
Domestic Policy in the Mid-1980s, ed. J. H. Moore* (Stanford, CA: Hoover Institution
Press, 1984), 23. Specifically, he suggested that the regulatory powers of the Fed
might be better housed within agencies like the FDIC or the comptroller of the
currency, while monetary policy could be conducted by the Treasury. Functions
like collecting data, monitoring reserve requirements, clearing checks, and issu-
ing currency could also be separated from monetary policy.

What Title XII does:

Title XII authorizes the Treasury to develop programs, including grants to financial institutions, to improve low- and moderate-income individuals' access to small-dollar loans and financial services.

It allows for government grants to community development financial institutions serving targeted investment areas for the purpose of establishing a reserve fund to compensate for the costs of a small-dollar loan program.

Why Title XII's approach is flawed:

Title XII facilitates direct government subsidization of banking services and underpricing of credit.

TITLE XII

Government Grant Programs

TITLE XII, "THE Improving Access to Mainstream Financial Institutions Act," does not respond to the financial crisis and, although well-intentioned, could undermine bank safety and soundness and harm the borrowers it is intended to help. The goal of Title XII is to encourage—including through subsidies—mainstream financial institutions' provision of services to low- and moderate-income individuals. It appears to be premised on an inaccurate set of assumptions about nonmainstream sources of financing. Moreover, by authorizing a new set of subsidies, it once again places taxpayer money at risk for bad loans made by the private sector.

Title XII authorizes the Treasury to develop multiyear programs of grants and agreements with financial institutions and governmental entities to (1) enable low- and moderate-income individuals to establish bank accounts and to improve their access to accounts on reasonable terms,[1] and (2) "provide low-cost, small loans to consumers that will provide alternatives to more costly small dollar loans."[2] In addition, Title XII allows grants to be made to community development financial institutions[3] and other financial institutions serving targeted investment areas for the purpose of establishing "a loan-loss reserve fund in order to defray the costs of a small dollar loan program."[4]

These programs entail direct government subsidization of the provision of banking services and set aside taxpayer money to cover losses on loans made by private entities. Financial institutions should not be encouraged to make loans that are not properly priced for the attendant risk. As the crisis illustrated, underpricing credit can harm both borrowers and financial institutions.

Instead of including Title XII in Dodd-Frank, the framers of the statute ought to have considered how regulatory requirements, including those imposed by Dodd-Frank, affect the ability of banks to serve lower-income consumers. Measures like the new limitations on debit interchange fees may increase the costs of services and decrease access to banking services by customers of modest means. One study estimated that the Fed's proposal for implementing the debit change regulations would have a dramatic impact on the number of unbanked people:

> As a result of the anticipated increase in banking fees, the number of unbanked individuals will increase. Fewer low-income households will continue to have checking accounts under the higher fees that will be imposed for these accounts. Accordingly, in the future, many low-income individuals will be induced to rely on check-cashing and other high-priced alternatives to traditional banking services. We do not have a reliable projection of the increase but we believe that it is plausible that the number of unbanked households could increase by more than one million and would argue that the Board should investigate this possible impact in more detail.[5]

In addition to interchange regulations, the new CFPB regulatory and enforcement regime could make access to credit more expensive. Dodd-Frank, by increasing regulatory costs for financial institutions of all sizes, is likely to raise the cost of banking services to consumers and make it more difficult for financial institutions to cater to lower-income individuals.

Title XII reflects an aversion to products that many Americans use rationally to meet emergency needs.[6] Title XII seeks to displace the providers of products like payday loans without demonstrating that the market is failing consumers.[7] Payday loans, although expensive to compensate for the risk the lender is taking, serve a legitimate purpose for borrowers in times of trouble.[8] As Zywicki notes in his comprehensive study of payday lending and alternatives, "Scholars have found that access to payday loans even can serve an important role in improving consumer welfare and quality of life."[9] By contrast, "many payday-lending consumers have had relatively negative experiences with traditional financial institutions."[10] Banks are free to compete with payday lenders by offering prudent, profitable, lower-cost alternatives to consumers. Subsidizing lower-cost alternatives to payday lending, however, simply moves the credit risk from lenders to taxpayers.

Title XII's goal of expanding access to credit for low- and moderate-income borrowers is commendable, but its method of achieving it—government subsidies—could give rise to harmful distortions in the market.

NOTES

1. *Dodd-Frank Wall Street Reform and Consumer Protection Act*, § 1204(a).
2. Ibid., § 1205(a).
3. A community development financial institution is an entity that meets certain criteria, including having "a primary mission of promoting community development," "provid[ing] development services in conjunction with equity investments or loans," and "maintain[ing], through representation on its governing board or otherwise, accountability to residents of its investment area or targeted population." *U.S. Code* 12, § 4702(5).
4. *Dodd-Frank Wall Street Reform and Consumer Protection Act*, § 1206, adding *U.S.*

Code 12, § 4719(b). Nonfederal matching funds equal to 50 percent of the grant are required.

5. David S. Evans, Robert E. Litan, and Richard Schmalensee, "Economic Analysis of the Effects of the Federal Reserve Board's Proposed Debit Card Interchange Fee Regulations on Consumers and Small Businesses," Fed Consumer Impact Study, February 22, 2011, 4, http://www.federalreserve.gov/SECRS/2011/March/20110308/R-1404/R-1404_030811_69120_621655419027_1.pdf.

6. According to the FDIC, "In 2011, 42.9 percent of US households had ever used one or more of the following types of AFS [alternative financial services] at some point in the past: non-bank check cashing, non-bank remittances, payday loans, pawn shops, rent-to-own stores, or refund anticipation loans." FDIC, "2011 FDIC National Survey of Unbanked and Underbanked Households," September 2012, 29, http://www.fdic.gov/householdsurvey/2012_unbankedreport.pdf. The FDIC found that convenience was the most cited reason for using non-bank check cashing and non-bank remittances. Households use payday loans and pawn shops, "because it is easier to get payday loans or to get money from a pawn shop than to qualify for a bank loan." Ibid., 37.

7. For an argument that the market is not failing, see Todd J. Zywicki, "The Case against New Restrictions on Payday Lending" (working paper no. 09-28, Mercatus Center at George Mason University, Arlington, VA, July 2009), 28, http://mercatus.org/sites/default/files/publication/WP0928_Payday%20Lending.pdf. Zywicki writes, "It is highly unlikely that there is a systematic market failure in the payday-lending market. The market is highly competitive: The number of payday-loan outlets has grown dramatically over the past decade, and payday lenders appear to compete aggressively for customers. Barriers to entry are low."

8. See, for example, Adair Morse, "Payday Lenders: Heroes or Villains?" *Journal of Financial Economics* 102 (2011): 28, 41. Morse writes that "among those individuals going to payday lenders following a financial shock (a personal emergency or natural disaster), lenders have a large mitigating effect in helping these individuals catch up with their obligations before facing foreclosure."

9. Zywicki, "The Case against New Restrictions on Payday Lending," 26.

10. Ibid., 25.

What Title XIII does:

Title XIII requires proceeds from sales of government-sponsored enterprise (GSE) obligations and securities and left-over stimulus funds to go to the Treasury.

It reduces the size of the Troubled Asset Relief Program.

It requires the Federal Housing Finance Agency (FHFA) to submit a report to Congress on its plans with respect to housing finance.

Why Title XIII's approach is flawed:

The inclusion of Title XIII masks Dodd-Frank's true cost.

It does not fully end TARP.

It does little to address GSE conservatorship, a significant crisis-era intervention.

TITLE XIII

Recouping Costs of Government Programs

T ITLE XIII OF Dodd-Frank, "The Pay It Back Act," contains a number of miscellaneous provisions but is predominantly focused on reining in previous government rescue efforts. It was likely included in Dodd-Frank because of its budgetary impact.

Title XIII required proceeds from sales of government-sponsored enterprise (GSE) obligations and securities and left-over stimulus funds to go to the Treasury for deficit reduction.[1] Title XIII also reduced the size of the Troubled Asset Relief Program (TARP), pursuant to which the government and other entities were bailed out during the crisis.[2] The addition of this provision improved Dodd-Frank's budgetary impact.[3] Nevertheless, TARP is still in existence and will be for some time. Many of the entities that received TARP money have yet to repay it.[4] Some entities that have repaid have done so with funds from another government program.[5] Arguments that taxpayers will be repaid in full or make a profit under TARP[6] ignore the opportunity cost of the billions that the Treasury poured into companies when other lenders would have charged much more to compensate for the risk of lending to uncertain entities in uncertain times.

The one forward-looking provision of Title XIII required the director of the Federal Housing Finance Agency (FHFA) to submit a report to Congress on the agency's plans "to continue to support and maintain the Nation's vital housing industry, while at the same time guaranteeing that the American taxpayer will not suffer unnecessary losses."[7] Along with a Title X provision that required the Treasury and the Department of Housing and Urban Development (HUD) to study "the options for ending the conservatorship of [Fannie Mae and Freddie Mac], while minimizing the cost to taxpayers,"[8] the FHFA study provision provided an excuse for the authors of Dodd-Frank to defer looking at issues central to the crisis. Although both studies were completed, no action has been taken to reform housing finance.[9]

The failure to address housing finance in Dodd-Frank and the continued reluctance to take up the issue in any meaningful way are not surprising in light of the many forces aligned against reform. Realtors, home builders, investors in mortgage-backed securities, advocates of affordable housing, and others consistently join forces to defeat substantive change and to argue that a central government role in housing finance is essential.[10]

Title XIII took a small step toward winding down the TARP and stimulus programs, but it did nothing substantive to address another crisis-era intervention—GSE conservatorship. Title XIV, which is specifically focused on the mortgage market, likewise fails to take substantive steps toward reforming mortgage finance and rolling back the government's involvement in the mortgage markets.

NOTES

1. *Dodd-Frank Wall Street Reform and Consumer Protection Act*, §§ 1304 and 1306.
2. Ibid., § 1302.
3. Congressional Budget Office, "CBO Estimate of the Net Deficit Effects of H.R. 4173, the Dodd-Frank Wall Street Reform and Consumer Protection Act," June 29, 2010, http://www.cbo.gov/sites/default/files/cbofiles/ftpdocs/116xx/doc11601/hr4173a

mendment.pdf. The Congressional Budget Office "estimated deficit reduction of $11 billion for fiscal year 2010 would stem from changes in the Troubled Asset Relief Program, created by the Emergency Economic Stabilization Act."

4. As of September 30, 2012, for example, there were still 290 banks in TARP's Capital Purchase Program. Department of the Treasury, Troubled Asset Relief Program Monthly Report to Congress, September 2012, 112th Cong., 2d sess. (Washington, DC, October 10, 2012), 7, http://www.treasury.gov/initiatives/financial-stability /reports/Documents/September%202012%20Monthly%20Report.pdf.

5. For example, 137 banks repaid TARP funds with funds from the Small Business Lending Fund. Ibid., 4.

6. See, for example, Department of the Treasury, "Financial Crisis Response in Charts" (slideshow, April 2012), 12, http://www.slideshare.net/USTreasuryDept/20120413 -financial-crisisresponse. The Treasury Department explained that "overall, the government is now expected to break even on its financial stability programs and may realize a positive return."

7. *Dodd-Frank Wall Street Reform and Consumer Protection Act,* § 1305.

8. Ibid., § 1074.

9. FHFA, *2011 Report to Congress,* 112th Cong., 2d sess. (Washington, DC, June 13, 2012), http://www.fhfa.gov/webfiles/24009/FHFA_RepToCongr11_6_14_508.pdf. The study by the Treasury and HUD described, with little detail, three potential options for reform. Department of Housing and Urban Development and Department of the Treasury, *Reforming America's Housing Finance Market: A Report to Congress,* 112th Cong., 1st sess. (February 2011), http://portal.hud.gov/hudportal /documents/huddoc?id=housingfinmarketreform.pdf.

10. But see Satya Thallam (ed.), *House of Cards: Reforming America's Housing Finance System* (Arlington, VA: Mercatus Center at George Mason University, February 2012), 67, http://mercatus.org/publication/house-cards. The publication offers substantive suggestions for reforming the mortgage-finance system.

What Title XIV does:

Title XIV requires mortgages to be consistent with borrowers' ability to repay, understandable, and not unfair, deceptive, or abusive.

It establishes the "qualified mortgage," a loan that meets specific criteria and is presumed to meet the ability-to-repay standard.

It introduces additional mortgage-market requirements.

It facilitates emergency housing-assistance programs.

Why Title XIV's approach is flawed:

Title XIV fails to address the elephant in the room: the dominant role of the government in mortgage financing.

It is likely to make mortgage financing more expensive.

It will likely result in a one-size-fits-all mortgage market with little flexibility to adjust terms to best fit borrowers' circumstances.

It gives regulators the power to pick and choose mortgage products for consumers.

The CFPB has failed to complete its rulemaking on the qualified mortgage, which leaves great uncertainty in the market.

TITLE XIV
Mortgages

ITLE XIV OF Dodd-Frank deals with residential mortgages.
In this sense, it is responsive to the financial crisis, during
which troubles in the mortgage market played such a large
role. Title XIV, however, fails to get to the root of the problems in the
mortgage market. Instead, it threatens to add to consumers' difficulties in financing their home purchases and perpetuates the government's outsized role in that area of the economy.

As noted above, Title XIV does not substantively address the
GSEs, Fannie Mae and Freddie Mac. Title XIV contains only a toothless "sense of Congress" provision, which recognizes the role that the
GSEs played in the subprime mortgage market and the importance
of GSE reform:

> It is the sense of the Congress that efforts to enhance by the
> protection, limitation, and regulation of the terms of residential mortgage credit and the practices related to such credit
> would be incomplete without enactment of meaningful structural reforms of Fannie Mae and Freddie Mac.[1]

Yet, without accompanying substantive reforms, such aspirational language has no effect. In fact, the housing finance market is
moving toward greater reliance on the government's involvement in
the mortgage market. As FHFA director Edward J. DeMarco recently

explained, "Today, the government touches more than 9 out of every 10 mortgages. In practical terms, this means that taxpayers are accountable for 90 percent of mortgages in this country."[2]

By focusing on measures intended to shield consumers from mortgage terms that regulators deem to be bad, Title XIV fails to address the root cause of mortgage abuses. Lax underwriting standards were a symptom of the government-backed mortgage-finance system and the government-encouraged emphasis on increasing homeownership.[3] The symptoms can best be addressed by using market mechanisms to make the institutions that decide to extend credit face the consequences of their decisions and by allowing individuals to decide for themselves whether to make the sacrifices necessary to buy a home and how best to finance that purchase.[4]

In the future, consumers will likely find it more difficult to obtain the mortgages they need. Some of the increased expense and difficulty will likely stem from the industry's more rigorous underwriting standards, which are consistent with prudent lending. Some of the added expense, though, will come from Title XIV's changes to the mortgage market in the name of protecting customers. These changes include new disclosure requirements, a prohibition on steering incentives, new requirements for high-risk mortgages, and new requirements for mortgage originators. Most significantly, Title XIV places the onus—couched in ambiguous statutory language—on mortgage lenders to make sure that consumers are neither offered[5] nor receive loans they cannot repay.

Title XIV establishes a "qualified mortgage," which is a loan that is presumed to satisfy the ability-to-repay criterion.[6] Qualified mortgages are supposed to be "structurally safer and pose lower risk for borrowers," than other mortgages, and "are underwritten according to standards that make it reasonable to expect that borrowers have an ability to repay."[7] The statute sets out characteristics for qualified mortgages, including a prohibition on terms longer than 30 years, a prohibition on interest-only payments, and income and asset verification requirements.[8] The CFPB has great discretion in departing from or adding to these criteria to craft the qualified mortgage.[9]

There is an intense debate about the appropriate parameters for qualified mortgages. Whatever parameters are chosen are expected to be important in defining the mortgage market. Observers anticipate that, given the consequences for violating the ability-to-repay requirement,[10] most future mortgages will be qualified mortgages.[11] The importance is magnified by the stipulation that the qualified residential mortgage, a separate safe harbor from risk-retention requirements being developed by the banking regulators and the SEC,[12] shall "be no broader than the definition 'qualified mortgage.'"[13] It remains to be seen how the CFPB will define qualified mortgages, but, as the financial crisis illustrated, the government is not good at balancing the conflicting goals of sound underwriting and broad access to credit.[14]

Another problem with Title XIV stems from its emphasis on regulatory approval of residential mortgage terms and practices. Regulators are directed to prohibit or condition mortgage terms, acts, or practices they determine to be abusive, unfair, deceptive, or predatory.[15] Government regulators, armed with the authority to prohibit certain types of mortgages, become the arbiters of the mortgages consumers can obtain. A possible result of this title is one-size-fits-all regulations or regulations that prohibit certain consumers from obtaining certain types of products.[16] A consumer who wants a 10-year mortgage, for example, may find himself forced into the 15- or 30-year mortgage regulators prefer. A person who plans to stay in his house for only five years might prefer a mortgage with an adjustable interest rate to a 30-year fixed-rate mortgage. The real message Title XIV sends to consumers is that the government has blessed all the mortgage products on the market as appropriate and consumer friendly. Assuming the government has signed off, consumers will be less likely to read Dodd-Frank's revamped disclosure to decide which mortgage products work best for them.[17]

Title XIV's grant programs related to housing only further the federal government's involvement in the market. HUD received access to $1 billion for emergency assistance to homeowners and was authorized to give up to $50,000 of assistance per homeowner.[18] An additional $1 billion was made available for state and local governments through HUD's Neighborhood Stabilization Program.[19] A third provision of Title XIV set up a legal program to provide money to organizations providing legal assistance to homeowners and tenants affected by foreclosure.[20] While well-intentioned, these provisions rely on bureaucratic interventions, which are difficult to design and implement effectively and efficiently.

If Title XIV helps consumers better understand mortgage terms and avoid mortgages that are not right for them, it will have achieved a laudable goal. Unfortunately, Title XIV also gives regulators the ability to block products they do not like and adds complex, ambiguous rules to the mortgage-lending business that will drive up costs for consumers and decrease their choices. Dodd-Frank should have focused its efforts instead on sensibly reforming housing finance. Sound underwriting practices—good for both consumers and financial institutions—would have followed.

NOTES

1. *Dodd-Frank Wall Street Reform and Consumer Protection Act*, § 1491(b).
2. Edward J. DeMarco, "The Conservatorships of Fannie Mae and Freddie Mac" (speech, National Association of Federal Credit Unions Congressional Caucus, Washington, DC, September 13, 2012), 6, http://www.fhfa.gov/web files/24489/2012_FHFA_-_NAFCU_Speech_final.pdf.
3. See, for example, Peter J. Wallison, "Dissenting Statement to the Report of the Financial Crisis Inquiry Commission," January 2011, 444, http://fcic-static.law

.stanford.edu/cdn_media/fcic-reports/fcic_final_report_wallison_dissent.pdf. Wallison explains that "the sine qua non of the financial crisis was US government housing policy, which led to the creation of 27 million subprime and other risky loans—half of all mortgages in the United States—which were ready to default as soon as the massive 1997–2007 housing bubble began to deflate. If the US government had not chosen this policy path—fostering the growth of a bubble of unprecedented size and an equally unprecedented number of weak and high risk residential mortgages—the great financial crisis of 2008 would never have occurred." See also Edward Glaeser, "Foreword," in *House of Cards,* 3. Glaeser writes, "Accompanied by the borrowing subsidy created by the Home Mortgage Interest Deduction and rule changes that enabled home buyers to obtain a loan with just a minimal down payment, GSE policies subsidized leverage and encouraged Americans to borrow as much as possible to bet on the vicissitudes of the housing market. During the boom, all this home buying was lauded for creating an 'ownership society.' Now, it appears that these policies actually seem to have helped create a foreclosure society."

4. As Sanders and Lea point out, the United States' housing-finance system is an outlier, both because it relies so heavily on GSEs and because of the limited consumer choices as reflected in the homogeneity of its mortgages. Michael Lea and Anthony B. Sanders, "The Future of Fannie Mae and Freddie Mac," in *House of Cards.*

5. It is difficult to understand the harm a consumer will suffer by merely being *offered* a loan she does not have the ability to repay.

6. *Dodd-Frank Wall Street Reform and Consumer Protection Act,* § 1412. The Fed, uncertain about what the framers of Dodd-Frank intended, proposed two alternatives, one in which the qualified mortgage would be a safe harbor and the other in which it would serve only as a rebuttable presumption of compliance with ability-to-repay requirements. Fed, "Regulation Z; Truth in Lending," Notice of Proposed Rulemaking, *Federal Register* 76 (May 11, 2011), 27390.

7. Raj Date, deputy director, CFPB, "Prepared Remarks at the Greenlining Institute Conference" (speech, Greenlining Institute Conference, Los Angeles, CA, April 20, 2012), http://www.consumerfinance.gov/speeches/prepared-remarks-by-raj -date-at-the-greenlining-institute-conference.

8. *Dodd-Frank Wall Street Reform and Consumer Protection Act,* § 1412.

9. Regardless of whether regulations under the title are implemented, Title XIV provisions will go into effect in January 2013. Ibid., § 1400(c). The Fed proposed a qualified mortgage rule before authority for the rulemaking transferred to the CFPB in July 2011. The CFPB recently reopened the comment period with respect to the rule but plans to have a rule finalized by January 2013. See CFPB, "Truth in Lending (Regulation Z)," Notice of Reopening of Comment Period and Request for Comment, *Federal Register* 77 (June 5, 2012), 33120.

10. Dodd-Frank section 1413 makes an ability-to-repay violation a defense against foreclosure. In addition to being more vulnerable to a foreclosure defense, non-qualified mortgages have certain limitations. For example, they cannot include prepayment penalties and cannot qualify for an exemption from the risk-retention requirements. *Dodd-Frank Wall Street Reform and Consumer Protection Act,* §§ 1414 and 941. Moreover, compliance with the ability-to-repay standard is likely to be made more difficult by the fact that state attorneys general are authorized, along with federal regulators, to enforce the standard. Ibid., § 1422. Multiple enforcers will add to the ambiguity of the standard.

11. See, for example, Raymond Natter, "Congressional Intent Regarding the Qualified Mortgage Provision," *Bloomberg-BNA Banking Report* 91 (May 25, 2012), 921, text following note 6. Natter anticipates that "As a practical matter, faced with the adverse consequences of making a non-QM loan . . . very few non-QM mortgages will be made."

12. For a discussion of QRMs, see the commentary on Title IX.

13. *Dodd-Frank Wall Street Reform and Consumer Protection Act,* § 941, which adds *U.S. Code* 15, § 78o-11(e)(4)(C).

14. Title XIV includes a reminder that nothing the CFPB does should be "construed as requiring a depository institution to apply mortgage underwriting standards that do not meet the minimum underwriting standards required by the appropriate prudential regulator." Ibid., § 1411(a). Nevertheless, because the CFPB does not have safety and soundness responsibilities, it may have an especially difficult time drawing a proper balance.

15. Ibid., § 1405, which adds *U.S. Code* 15, § 1639b(e).

16. Presumably, the CFPB will interpret the term "abusive" in this context in a similar manner to its interpretation of "abusive" under its authority to prohibit abusive acts or practices in connection with consumer financial transactions under Dodd-Frank (Ibid., § 1031). One commentator, walking through possibilities of how the CFPB might interpret "abusive" under § 1031, suggested that particular contract terms could be banned, borrowers in certain classes could be precluded from using certain products, or products could be banned altogether. See Zywicki, "The Consumer Financial Protection Bureau," 68–71.

17. The CFPB recently announced its proposed new mortgage disclosure form. See, for example, CFPB, "Integrated Mortgage Disclosures under the Real Estate Settlement Procedures Act (Regulation X) and the Truth in Lending Act (Regulation Z)," Notice of Proposed Rulemaking, *Federal Register* 77 (August 23, 2012), 51116.

18. *Dodd-Frank Wall Street Reform and Consumer Protection Act,* § 1496.

19. Ibid., § 1497.

20. Ibid., § 1498.

What Title XV does:

Title XV requires companies to publicly disclose their use of conflict minerals from the Democratic Republic of the Congo (DRC) and adjoining countries and the measures, including an independent audit, they have taken to determine whether the minerals are conflict free.

It directs the State Department to come up with a strategy to address the connection between conflict minerals and violence in the DRC.

It requires that companies disclose mine safety violations identified by the Mine Safety and Health Administration in their SEC filings.

It requires companies engaged in the commercial development of oil, gas, or minerals to disclose payments made to foreign governments to further commercial-development activities.

Why Title XV's approach is flawed:

Title XV requires the SEC to regulate in delicate areas about which it is has no expertise.

It distracts the SEC from undertaking reforms to prevent future financial crises.

It reflects a stark departure from the SEC's investor-oriented disclosure tradition.

The conflict minerals provision will be extremely expensive and could end up harming the victims of violence in the DRC it intends to help.

Resource-extraction disclosure threatens capital formation in the United States and will likely place US firms at a competitive disadvantage.

TITLE XV

Requirements for Nonfinancial Companies

T ITLE XV, "MISCELLANEOUS Provisions," has more to do with foreign policy than the financial crisis. This portion of Dodd-Frank focuses primarily on public-company disclosures regarding conflict minerals, mine safety, and resource extraction.[1] Title XV continues a disturbing trend of using the SEC and its public disclosures to meet the needs of groups other than investors or potential investors.[2] Moreover, Title XV requires the SEC to become the regulator of matters far outside its area of expertise. As a result, Title XV not only fails to address any issues that arose during the financial crisis, but it also distracts the SEC from undertaking reforms designed to prevent future financial crises.

The SEC's mission is protecting investors; maintaining fair, orderly, and efficient markets; and facilitating capital formation. Generally, the SEC has not told investors in which companies they should or should not invest. Instead, the SEC has allowed investors to make their own investment decisions while requiring companies that sell their shares publicly to make disclosures so investors and potential investors can make rational investment decisions. The SEC explains the principle behind its disclosure approach as follows:

The laws and rules that govern the securities industry in the United States derive from a simple and straightforward concept: all investors, whether large institutions or private individuals, should have access to certain basic facts about an investment prior to buying it, and so long as they hold it. To achieve this, the SEC requires public companies to disclose meaningful financial and other information to the public. This provides a common pool of knowledge for all investors to use to judge for themselves whether to buy, sell, or hold a particular security. Only through the steady flow of timely, comprehensive, and accurate information can people make sound investment decisions.[3]

A fundamental tenet of the SEC's disclosure regime is the idea that investors do not want to know every detail about a company; rather, they want only information material to their investment decisions. In order not to inundate investors with irrelevant details, companies are generally not required to disclose immaterial information.[4] Because some investors care more about certain issues than others, the materiality standard turns on what a reasonable investor would consider important.[5]

Title XV requires disclosures in three new areas: conflict minerals, mine safety, and payments by resource-extraction issuers. None of these disclosures fits within the above-described SEC investor-oriented disclosure tradition. Instead, they reflect the interests of noninvestor groups and depart from the SEC's standard disclosure principles. The advocates of the Title XV disclosures perceived Dodd-Frank as an opportune, if not particularly pertinent, vehicle for achieving their objectives.

Section 1502 applies to companies that use coltan, cassiterite, gold, wolframite, their derivatives, or any other mineral or its derivative determined by the Secretary of State to be financing conflict in the Democratic Republic of the Congo (DRC).[6] Such minerals are used to produce, among other things, electronics, jewelry, and aerospace products.[7] Affected companies would have to disclose annually whether they use minerals from the DRC or an adjoining country. Companies are required to prepare a report describing due-diligence measures—including an independent audit—on the source and chain of custody of those minerals. Accordingly, companies throughout the supply chain will bear costs. The costs of section 1502 are expected to be high, perhaps in the multibillions of dollars.[8]

Despite the large costs, the SEC adopted a rule that is arguably even more onerous than the statute requires.[9] For example, the SEC chose not to exempt small issuers. Further, the SEC's rule does not include a de minimis threshold—"even minute or trace amounts of a conflict mineral could trigger disclosure obligations."[10] In addition, although the SEC proposed that conflict mineral disclosures be furnished rather than filed, it adopted a filing requirement, which exposes companies to greater legal liability.

In the end, the conflict minerals provision could make the situation in the DRC worse, not better.[11] As the SEC admits, section 1502 was intended to stop violence and create peace in the DRC:

> and [it] is not necessarily intended to generate measurable, direct economic benefits to investors or issuers specifically. Additionally, the social benefits are quite different from the economic or investor protection benefits that our rules ordinarily strive to achieve. We therefore have not attempted to quantify the benefits of the final rule.

The SEC, with its lack of expertise in foreign-policy responses to humanitarian crises, cannot be expected to have figured out without outside input how its rules would affect the DRC. According to some observers, however, the SEC failed to give due consideration to the views of people on the ground in the DRC.[12] Even before the SEC had finalized its rules, changes in the DRC began.[13] Professor Laura E. Seay explains that "section 1502 has inadvertently and directly negatively affected up to 5–12 million Congolese citizens. Many miners cannot feed their children, their children are not in school this year because they cannot pay tuition fees, and those who are ill cannot afford medical treatment."[14] The potential that the suffering in the DRC will increase is one of the most troubling potential unintended consequences of Dodd-Frank.

Section 1503 requires companies to disclose mine safety violations identified by the Mine Safety and Health Administration in their SEC filings. Certain notices from the administration require immediate SEC filings on Form 8-K. This requirement was added in response to the April 2010 tragedy at the Upper Big Branch Mine in West Virginia rather than in response to concerns about inadequate disclosure.[15] It "runs the risk of creating unnecessary 'noise' in the public reporting for issuers operating mines."[16] Understandable despair at the loss of life in mining accidents has led to a solution that benefits neither miners nor investors.

Section 1504 of Dodd-Frank requires companies engaged in the commercial development of oil, gas, or minerals to disclose payments they make to foreign governments to further their commercial-development activities. The SEC strained to find benefits to investors in the new section 1504 disclosure but acknowledged that those benefits were incidental to Congress's purpose of "the accountability of governments to their citizens in resource-rich countries for the wealth generated by those resources."[17] As a United States Agency for International Development (USAID) official explained, section 1504 is a foreign policy tool:

> The enforcement of the proposed rules contributes towards
> U.S. Government foreign policy goals of supporting stable

156

and democratic governments, with a particular emphasis on USAID's role in providing assistance to resource-rich countries in support of economic growth, good governance, transparency, and building civil society.[18]

The need for this provision, even for foreign policy purposes, is puzzling given that there is already a voluntary international initiative aimed at addressing these same issues. The Extractive Industries Transparency Initiative brings together governments, companies, and others to enhance the transparency of payments to foreign governments.[19]

Not only is section 1504 driven by objectives beyond the scope of the SEC's mission, it actually conflicts directly with those objectives. It threatens to harm capital formation in the United States. Moreover, companies subject to the provision may face a competitive disadvantage among foreign rivals.[20] As SEC commissioner Daniel Gallagher explains,

> As an independent agency, the SEC should have played a significant role in informing Congress about the pitfalls of mandating rulemakings that are not germane to our mission. In providing that advice, the Commission would make it clear when such mandates conflict with our mission, as well as our well-established obligation to conduct a thorough cost-benefit analysis in our rulemakings. With respect to Section 1504 in particular, the SEC would stress that in Section 23 of the Exchange Act, Congress prohibited us from promulgating rules—such as the rule we promulgate today—that burden competition for a purpose not necessary or appropriate in furtherance of the purposes of the Exchange Act. Assuming those discussions occurred, they obviously were unsuccessful—hence, our two-year-plus struggle with the Section 1504 mandate.[21]

Gallagher went on to explain how the provision and the SEC's discretionary choices in implementing it create competitive imbalances and "risk violating host country law—which may . . . include national security laws not specific to the extractive industries."[22]

Title XV of Dodd-Frank offers a clear example of how a statute invoked as the answer to the financial crisis is, in reality, an odd conglomeration of responses to issues, many of which had nothing to do with the financial crisis. As the SEC struggles to recover from its recent investor-protection failures, statutory mandates that expand its protective net far beyond the US securities markets do not help.

NOTES

1. Title XV also includes a provision related to International Monetary Fund loans, a requirement that the GAO conduct a study on inspectors general, and a requirement that the FDIC conduct a study on core deposits and brokered deposits. This commentary does not address these provisions.

2. David Lynn's excellent article on this subject points out that Title XV is not the first instance of the SEC's being used to further policy goals rather than to undertake its traditional disclosure objectives. He points to the SEC's Office of Global Security Risk and the SEC's shareholder proposal process. David M. Lynn, "The Dodd-Frank Act's Specialized Corporate Disclosure: Using the Securities Laws to Address Public Policy Issues," *Journal of Business and Technology Law* 6 (2011): 327, 350–54. There are other examples of SEC disclosures that appear to be motivated by the interests of noninvestors, rather than the needs of investors. See, for example, SEC, "Commission Guidance Regarding Disclosure Related to Climate Change," Interpretation, *Federal Register* 75 (February 8, 2010), 6290.

3. SEC, "The Investor's Advocate: How the SEC Protects Investors, Maintains Market Integrity, and Facilitates Capital Formation," October 12, 2012, http://www.sec.gov /about/whatwedo.shtml.

4. *TSC Industries v. Northway,* 426 U.S. 438, 448-49 (1976). The court explained that "Some information is of such dubious significance that insistence on its disclosure may accomplish more harm than good. . . . if the standard of materiality is unnecessarily low, not only may the corporation and its management be subjected to liability for insignificant omissions or misstatements, but also management's

fear of exposing itself to substantial liability may cause it simply to bury the share-holders in an avalanche of trivial information—a result that is hardly conducive to informed decisionmaking."

5. See Ibid., 449. The court established the standard that "an omitted fact is material if there is a substantial likelihood that a reasonable shareholder would consider it important in deciding how to vote. . . . under all the circumstances, the omitted fact would have assumed actual significance in the deliberations of the reasonable shareholder. Put another way, there must be a substantial likelihood that the disclosure of the omitted fact would have been viewed by the reasonable investor as having significantly altered the 'total mix' of information made available." See also *Basic v. Levinson,* 485 U.S. 224, 249 (1988), which adopted *TSC Industries'* standard in the antifraud context.

6. *Dodd-Frank Wall Street Reform and Consumer Protection Act,* § 1502(c), also includes directives for the Secretary of State, including developing, within 180 days of Dodd-Frank's passage, a peace and security plan for the Democratic Republic of the Congo and a plan to help companies in their due diligence activities pursuant to § 1502.

7. The rule's reach goes far beyond these products. See, for example, SEC, "Roundtable on Conflict Minerals," October 18, 2011, http://www.sec.gov/spotlight/con flictminerals/conflictmineralsroundtable101811-transcript.txt. Irma Villarreal of Kraft Foods commented, "When the Commission issued its proposed rules, many companies, including mine, were surprised that the disclosure requirements would apply to them. Because we may use tin in some of our packaging for our biscuits, cookies and coffee, for example, we are subject to the rules."

8. A Tulane University study that looked at costs to directly affected companies and their first-tier suppliers estimated costs to be $7.93 billion. Chris Bayer, "A Critical Analysis of the SEC and NAM Economic Impact Models and the Proposal of a 3rd Model in View of Implementation of Section 1502 of the 2010 Dodd-Frank Wall Street Reform and Consumer Protection Act," Tulane University Law School, Payson Center for International Development, October 17, 2011, http://www.sec.gov /comments/s7-40-10/s74010-351.pdf. See also Stephen Jacobs, "Comment Letter," National Association of Manufacturers, March 2, 2011, 23. NAM explained, "Based on discussions with member companies the NAM's estimate of the cost to manufacturers of complying with the draft rule would be $9.4 billion ($8 billion for issuers and $1.4 billion from smaller companies that are not issuers). As an alternative methodology, we also extrapolated from the recent experience of company costs in complying with the European Union's hazardous waste directive, and estimated on that basis that the economic impact of the SEC's proposed regulations could be as high as $16 billion." The SEC estimated initial compliance costs of $3 to $4 billion. See SEC, "Conflict Minerals," Notice of Final Rulemaking, *Federal Register*

77 (September 12, 2012), 56274, 56353. These cost estimates are not directly comparable to one another, given the different factors each group looked at, but there is widespread agreement that the rule is likely to impose heavy costs.

9. SEC, "Conflict Minerals," Notice of Final Rulemaking. For a discussion of areas in which the SEC made policy choices that increased, rather than decreased, costs, see Daniel M. Gallagher, "Statement at SEC Open Meeting: Proposed Rule to Implement Section 1502 of the Dodd-Frank Act—the 'Conflict Minerals' Provision" (speech, SEC, Washington, DC, August 22, 2012), http://www.sec.gov/news/speech/2012/spch082212dmg-minerals.htm.

10. SEC, "Conflict Minerals," Notice of Final Rulemaking, 56298.

11. Troy A. Paredes, "Statement at Open Meeting to Adopt a Final Rule Regarding Conflict Minerals Pursuant to Section 1502 of the Dodd-Frank Act" (speech, SEC, Washington, DC, August 22, 2012), http://www.sec.gov/news/speech/2012/spch082212tap-minerals.htm. Paredes said, "We all want the violence in the DRC to end. Unfortunately, the adopting release does not offer a reasoned basis for concluding that the final rule will help bring this about, and there is cause for concern that the hardship and suffering could worsen if the outcome is a de facto embargo. Accordingly, I caution against any sense that the need for action to abate the humanitarian crisis is allayed because of the rule the Commission is adopting today."

12. See, for example, House Committee on Financial Services, Subcommittee on International Policy and Trade, *The Costs and Consequences of Dodd-Frank Section 1502: Impacts on America and the Congo*, 112th Cong., 2d sess. (May 10, 2012) (statement of Mvemba P. Dizolele), 3, http://financialservices.house.gov/UploadedFiles/HHRG-112-BA20-WState-MDizolele-20120510.pdf. Dizolele, a visiting fellow at the Hoover Institution, testified that "the Congolese have been excluded from the policy discussion around Section 1502. Their exclusion is such an accepted norm that no Congolese was invited to speak at the Securities Exchange Commission Public Roundtable on Dodd-Frank 1502 on October 18, 2011 here in Washington, DC. The Congolese experts who had traveled for the event were confined to their seats in the auditorium, listening to Western activists and corporations debate the fate of Congo's resources. As it was at the Berlin Conference in 1885 when Western powers divided Africa, the primary stakeholders were simply excluded."

13. See generally Laura E. Seay, "What's Wrong With Dodd-Frank 1502? Conflict Minerals, Civilian Livelihoods, and the Unintended Consequences of Western Advocacy" (working paper 284, Center for Global Development, Washington, DC, January 2012), http://www.cgdev.org/files/1425843_file_Seay_Dodd_Frank_FINAL.pdf. See also SEC, "Roundtable on Conflict Minerals." Benedict Cohen, chief counsel of litigation of the Boeing Company, commented on "the immediate and startling reaction which occurred upon the enactment of the Dodd-Frank legislation on a virtual overnight, virtual complete embargo. Indeed there's some risk, I think; not

that there will be under compliance and insufficient disinvestment in conflict-affected mines, but a risk of over compliance and inappropriate disinvestments."

14. Seay, "What's Wrong With Dodd-Frank 1502?," text accompanying notes 33–34.

15. See, for example, Letter from Howard B. Dicker, chair, Securities Regulation Committee, New York Bar Association, to Elizabeth Murphy, secretary, SEC, March 1, 2011, http://www.sec.gov/comments/s7-41-10/s74110-23.pdf. Dicker observes that material mine health and safety issues would already have to be disclosed under existing SEC rules, so "in our view, Section 1503 is therefore best understood as focusing on other issues, and on dissemination of the required information to a broader audience, not limited to investors."

16. Lynn, "The Dodd-Frank Act's Specialized Corporate Disclosure," 345.

17. SEC, "Disclosure of Payments by Resource Extraction Issuers," Notice of Final Rulemaking, *Federal Register* 77 (September 12, 2012), 56365, 56398.

18. Letter from Eric G. Postel, assistant administrator, Bureau for Economic Growth, Agriculture, and Trade, USAID, to Elizabeth M. Murphy, secretary, SEC, July 15, 2011, http://www.sec.gov/comments/s7-42-10/s74210-101.pdf.

19. See Extractive Industries Transparency Initiative (EITI), "What Is the EITI?" website, http://eiti.org/eiti.

20. See, for example, Branden Carl Berns, "Will Oil and Gas Issuers Leave U.S. Equity Markets in Response to Section 1504 of the Dodd-Frank Act? Can They Afford Not To?" *Columbia Business Law Review* (2011): 758. Berns argues that, absent a way to expand the reach of the provision, US companies covered by section 1504 will be at a competitive disadvantage, and he predicts harm to US investors.

21. Daniel M. Gallagher, "Proposed Rules to Implement Section 1504 of the Dodd-Frank Act ('Disclosure of Payments by Resource Extraction Issuers')" (speech, SEC open meeting, Washington, DC, August 22, 2012), http://www.sec.gov/news/speech/2012/spch082212dmg-extraction.htm.

22. Ibid.

What Title XVI does:

Title XVI exempts particular derivatives from section 1256 tax treatment.

Why Title XVI's approach is flawed:

Title XVI could have meaningful revenue implications for the United States, although the nature and magnitude of those implications remains unclear.

TITLE XVI
Taxing Derivatives

ITLE XVI, THE final section of Dodd-Frank, is less than a page long. Even at that length, its implications remain uncertain. It relates to the tax treatment of certain derivatives products. Prior to Dodd-Frank, tax treatment for derivatives turned on whether they were traded on an exchange. Title VII of Dodd-Frank seeks to move many more derivatives onto exchanges. This raises questions about the tax treatment of derivatives formerly traded off-exchange. Title XVI addresses the issue by definitively carving some derivatives out from section 1256 tax treatment.[1]

Tax issues and derivatives issues can be quite complex on their own. The marriage of the two can prove to be even more difficult to understand. This is the case with Title XVI. As one commentator explained,

> At the very last hour of Dodd-Frank's marathon progress through Congress, this issue was partially addressed through the adoption of an amendment to § 1256 that clarifies that certain types of OTC swaps will not become subject to § 1256. Notwithstanding this amendment, many questions remain, as the scope of the amendment is not clear. In addition, decisions still to be made by regulators and the market as to how derivatives will be traded are likely to affect the impact of the amendment.[2]

Title XVI could end up helping corporate taxpayers, for whom section 1256 tax treatment is not as favorable as it tends to be for individual taxpayers.[3] Given the size of the derivatives market, the change could have meaningful revenue implications for the United States, although the nature and magnitude of those implications remains unclear.[4] As with many other aspects of Dodd-Frank, how Title XVI will work depends on how regulators exercise their considerable discretion in implementing the statute and how the market responds.

NOTES

1. The staff of the Joint Committee on Taxation explains the tax treatment as follows:

> In general, section 1256 requires taxpayers to treat each section 1256 contract as if it were sold (and repurchased) for its fair market value on the last day of the year (i.e., "marked to market"). Any gain or loss with respect to a section 1256 contract that is subject to the mark-to-market rule is treated as short-term capital gain or loss to the extent of 40 percent of the gain or loss, and long-term capital gain or loss to the extent of the remaining 60 percent of the gain or loss (the "60/40 rule").

Staff of the Joint Committee on Taxation, "A Report to the Joint Committee on Taxation: Present Law and Issues Related to the Taxation of Financial Instruments and Products" (report JCX-56-11, Washington, DC, December 2, 2011), 34–35, https://www.jct.gov/publications.html?func=startdown&id=4372.

2. Erika W. Nijenhuis, "New Tax Issues Arising from the Dodd-Frank Act and Related Changes to Market Practice for Derivatives," *Columbia Journal of Tax Law* 2 (2011): 1, 4. See also Staff of the Joint Committee on Taxation, "A Report to the Joint Committee on Taxation," 83. The Joint Committee on Taxation report points out that uncertainty related to Dodd-Frank and changes in the futures markets are "testing the boundaries of the term 'regulated futures contract' under section 1256." The Internal Revenue Service answered some questions about the effects of Title XVI. See Internal Revenue Service, "Swap Exclusion for Section 1256 Contracts," Notice of Proposed Rulemaking, *Federal Register* 76 (September 16, 2011), 57684.

3. See Staff of the Joint Committee on Taxation, "A Report to the Joint Committee on

Taxation," 82. The report explains the different effects of section 1256 tax treatment on individual and corporate taxpayers.

4. See, for example, letter from Douglas W. Elmendorf, director, Congressional Budget Office, to Christopher J. Dodd, chairman, Senate Committee on Banking, Housing, and Urban Affairs, May 3, 2010, http://www.cbo.gov/sites/default/files/cbofiles/ftpdocs/114xx/doc11476/s3217amendmt.pdf. The letter anticipates, before the addition of Title XVI, that taxpayers would use the Title VII changes with respect to derivatives trading and clearing to argue for section 1256 tax treatment, which would have an uncertain effect on revenues.

PART II
Perspectives on Dodd-Frank

The following essays offer the perspectives of four scholars on Dodd-Frank. The first two essays offer high-level assessments of the act by looking at it against its historical backdrop. These essays consider whether Dodd-Frank was a disciplined and comprehensive response to the admittedly complex and multifaceted crisis. The scholars consider approaches the drafters of Dodd-Frank could have taken and solutions they could have included in crafting an effective and comprehensive response to the crisis. These essays, while acknowledging the daunting challenges faced by the statute's drafters, identify ways in which Dodd-Frank was not as carefully crafted as it might have been. The final essay assesses Dodd-Frank's impact by employing RegData, a methodology that quantifies the impact of regulations by analyzing their content.

Dodd-Frank

The Good and the Not-So-Good

*by Lawrence J. White**

T HE DODD-FRANK WALL Street Reform and Consumer Protection Act of 2010 was clearly the most ambitious piece of financial-sector legislation since the 1930s. Passed in the wake of the financial crisis of 2008–2009, the act tried to remedy the failings that its authors perceived to have caused that financial crisis. Unfortunately, it also addresses a number of issues that had nothing to do with the crisis and fails to address one of the central questions raised by the crisis: What should be done about Fannie Mae and Freddie Mac—in essence, what should be the future structure of residential mortgage finance in the United States?

The Causes of the Crisis

Any assessment of Dodd-Frank must start with the assessor's perspective on the causes of the crisis.

---

* During 1986–1989, the author was a board member on the Federal Home Loan Bank Board with responsibilities that included being a board member of Freddie Mac.

At the center of the financial crisis of 2008–2009 was a housing boom—which, with hindsight, we now know to have been a bubble—that began in the late 1990s. Feeding that bubble was the widespread belief among the participants in the housing sector that housing prices always went up. Of course, if housing prices always went up, residential mortgages (and the securities structured from them) would rarely cause a problem. Even if the borrower lost her job or otherwise lost her repayment capabilities, she could always sell the house—usually at a profit, of course, since prices would always increase—and pay off the mortgage from the proceeds.

Widespread and broad-brush government policies that encouraged greater investment and consumption of housing (including support for Fannie Mae and Freddie Mac) contributed to the housing boom, as did excessively expansionary monetary policies over 2003–2004, when the Federal Reserve continued for too long to worry about the potential of deflation and the adverse effects that would follow.

As the housing boom progressed, lending standards loosened, and borrowers with increasingly doubtful abilities to repay mortgages (except through home resale at a profit) were granted increasingly doubtful mortgages. At least through mid-2006, though, housing prices continued to increase and mortgage default rates remained quite low. (Fannie Mae and Freddie Mac, for example, reported annual loss rates on the mortgages they held and securitized of 0.01 percent.) "Private-label" mortgage-backed securities (MBS) not guaranteed by Fannie or Freddie performed well (since the underlying mortgages performed well). The major credit rating agencies—whose favorable ratings were necessary (by regulation) for banks and other depository institutions, insurance companies, pension funds, broker-dealers, and money market mutual funds to be able to buy or invest in these securities—became increasingly optimistic about those securities' prospects, despite the deteriorating lending standards.

Housing prices did start to decline in mid-2006, and mortgage borrowers began to default. Then the MBS constructed from these shaky mortgages began to default and decline in value as well. It now appears that housing prices declined about 35 percent (as measured by the Case-Shiller index) from mid-2006 to mid-2012. Since aggregate housing value in mid-2006 was around $20 trillion (according to the Federal Reserve's "Flow of Funds" database), this has meant a $7 trillion decline in housing value. A housing-led recession for the US economy was unavoidable.

A financial crisis was not inevitable, however. What made the difference was the extremely thin capitalization, or extremely high leverage, of the financial sector. The following comparison of the effects of the collapse of the dot-com stock-market bubble of the late 1990s and the collapse of the housing bubble of the 2000s shows the importance of leverage in the more recent collapse.

Between year-end 1999 and year-end 2002, the aggregate stock-market value decreased about $6.5 trillion. This represented a massive loss of wealth for the US economy. The economy slowed and entered a recession in March 2001; however, the recession was comparatively mild and short. In essence, the loss of wealth was absorbed, and the economy moved on.

By contrast, the roughly comparable amount of housing-sector losses—$7 trillion—has had far more severe consequences for the US economy. Why the difference?

In the case of the bursting of the dot-com bubble, the losses were mostly absorbed by households in their own portfolios of stocks and equities-based mutual funds and through their pension funds' holding of equities. These were unleveraged vehicles. By contrast, although most of the housing-sector losses were again absorbed by households, about $1.5 trillion (slightly more than one-fifth) of the housing-sector losses entered the financial sector through losses on mortgages and losses on MBS. The highly leveraged financial sector, with some large financial institutions leveraged $33 in debt for every $1 of equity, could not absorb those losses. Lending ground to a halt, and the US economy entered a far more severe recession than had been the case seven years earlier.

To illustrate these thin capital levels (high leverage levels), Table 1 reproduces the asset sizes and net-worth percentages (since net worth is, approximately, capital for financial institutions) of the 15 largest US financial institutions for year-end 2007, just prior to the onset of the crisis. It is clear that these very large institutions were ill-prepared to absorb significant losses.

The Good Things in Dodd-Frank

This short essay does not attempt to summarize all of the provisions of an 849-page piece of legislation. Instead, here I mention some of the more important good things in the act. In the following section I will discuss some of the more important not-so-good features of the act. There will be some major features of the bill (such as the creation of the Consumer Financial Protection Bureau and the Office of Financial Research) about which I don't have strong feelings. I leave those for others to characterize.

Emphasizing the Role of Capital. Prior to the onset of the crisis, the five large investment banks (Goldman Sachs, Morgan Stanley, Merrill Lynch, Lehman Brothers, and Bear Stearns), Fannie Mae and Freddie Mac, the holding company of Citigroup (which had about $0.9 trillion of Citi's $2.2 trillion in assets), and the Financial Products unit of AIG (which wrote hundreds of billions of dollars of insurance contracts on MBS without setting aside sufficient capital) were far too thinly capitalized. Although prudential regulation nominally applied to all of them, their prudential regulators did not or could

Table 1. Fifteen Largest Financial Institutions in the United States (by asset size, December 31, 2007)

Rank	Financial Institution	Category	Assets ($ billion)	Equity as Percentage of Assets
1	Citigroup	Commercial bank	$2,182	5.2%
2	Bank of America	Commercial bank	1,716	8.6
3	JPMorgan Chase	Commercial bank	1,562	7.9
4	Goldman Sachs	Investment bank	1,120	3.8
5	American International Group	Insurance conglomerate	1,061	9.0
6	Morgan Stanley	Investment bank	1,045	3.0
7	Merrill Lynch	Investment bank	1,020	3.1
8	Fannie Mae	GSE	883	5.0
9	Freddie Mac	GSE	794	3.4
10	Wachovia	Commercial bank	783	9.8
11	Lehman Brothers	Investment bank	691	3.3
12	Wells Fargo	Commercial bank	575	8.3
13	MetLife	Insurance	559	6.3
14	Prudential	Insurance	486	4.8
15	Bear Stearns	Investment bank	395	3.0

Note: The Federal Home Loan Bank System ($1,272) and TIAA-CREF ($420) have been excluded from this list. If GE Capital were a stand-alone finance company, its asset size ($650) would place it at number 12.
Source: "2008 Fortune 500," *Fortune* 157, no. 9 (May 5, 2008), http://money.cnn.com/magazines/fortune/fortune500/2008/snapshots/2255.html.

not require sufficient capital relative to the risks these institutions were undertaking.

Dodd-Frank emphasizes the role of capital in the future prudential regulation of financial institutions. This is all to its credit. Of course, it will be important that prudential regulators remain diligent and vigilant in the enforcement of higher capital levels.

Expanding Prudential Regulation to Encompass Large Systemic Financial Institutions. Recognizing the systemic nature of the financial crisis, Dodd-Frank creates a Financial Stability Oversight Council (FSOC) that is chaired by the Treasury secretary. The responsibilities of the FSOC include designating systemically important financial institutions (SIFIs) not already covered by prudential regulation. The SIFIs will be prudentially regulated by the Federal Reserve, including (of course) robust capital requirements.

Examples of SIFIs currently not subject to prudential regulation include large hedge funds, large financing subsidiaries of industrial corporations (for example, GE Capital, as per Table 1), large insurance holding companies, and major clearing and infrastructure institutions for financial instruments. It is possible that designating a financial institution as a SIFI might cause the financial markets to believe this institution would be too big to fail and that its creditors would therefore be bailed out if the institution encountered financial difficulties. In turn, this would cause the creditors to lend to the institution at favorable rates and give the institution an unwarranted competitive advantage. However, the eagerness of potential candidate institutions to avoid the SIFI designation appears to suggest the opposite: that the consequent prudential regulation will be onerous. In any event, implementation and enforcement will be crucial.

Orderly Liquidation Authority. The Federal Deposit Insurance Corporation (FDIC) acts as the receiver for insolvent depository institutions (except for credit unions, for which the National Credit Union Administration has a similar role). The FDIC's resolution process for these insolvent institutions is generally recognized as working smoothly, especially for small- and medium-size institutions.

However, prior to Dodd-Frank, the FDIC did not have receivership powers vis-à-vis nondepository financial institutions. Except for insurance companies (which are prudentially regulated by the states, which also have receivership powers vis-à-vis insolvent insurance companies), such financial institutions (if insolvent—that is, if their assets are inadequate to cover their liabilities) could be resolved only through bankruptcy. The bankruptcy of Lehman Brothers in September 2008 was highly disruptive to the financial markets, especially since it occurred at a time of high stress in the financial markets. The Lehman bankruptcy triggered a classic run by the short-term liability holders of the other investment banks and of bank holding companies, which also were not covered by FDIC deposit insurance or by the FDIC's resolution authority.

Dodd-Frank gives receivership powers—Orderly Liquidation Authority (OLA)—to the FDIC for insolvent SIFIs. Because there is no deposit insurance for the liabilities of SIFIs, the resolution process will be considerably more difficult. The FDIC's imposition of losses on creditors of an insolvent SIFI would likely inspire runs by short-term creditors of other similar SIFIs. Although the FDIC has not yet finalized all of its procedures for OLA, it appears to realize that a crucial piece of the process must be a (prudential regulatory) requirement that a SIFI's debt structure include a sufficiently large amount of long-term debt that can be converted into equity. Such debt is frequently described as "bail-in-able" debt, "contingent capital," or "subordinated" debt. In essence, the short-term creditors of an insolvent SIFI will be kept whole (and thus the short-term creditors at other SIFIs would be less likely to run), at the expense of the long-term (subordinated) creditors. Here, again, the actual execution of the FDIC's OLA authority will be crucial.

Reducing the Centrality of the Large Credit Rating Agencies. Prudential regulators' insistence (which began in 1936) that their regulated financial institutions heed the major credit-rating agencies' ratings elevated the agencies' importance to the financial sector. The financial institutions' heavy reliance on credit rating agencies when making choices as to bonds for investment magnified the consequences of rating agencies' errors in being too optimistic with respect to the creditworthiness of MBS with low-quality mortgages as collateral.

In an effort to reduce the centrality of ratings, Dodd-Frank repeals all statutory language that mandated the use of ratings and instructs regulators to eliminate the required use of ratings in their regulations. The Securities and Exchange Commission (SEC) initially moved faster in this respect, but has since bogged down and has yet (as of early November 2012) to issue final rules that would apply to bond investments by money market mutual funds or by broker-dealers; the bank regulators initially moved more slowly but issued final rules in the summer of 2012 that removed the required use of ratings with respect to banks' investments in bonds.

The Elimination of the Final Vestige of "Regulation Q." Although this provision of Dodd-Frank had no connection to the financial crisis, it nevertheless was a worthwhile step: The act repealed the last vestige of "Regulation Q"—the piece of the Banking Act of 1933 that had authorized the Federal Reserve to place ceilings on the rates banks could pay their depositors and that had mandated that banks could not pay interest on the checking accounts held by businesses. Although most of the Regulation Q authority to set maximum interest rates on deposits had been phased out in the early 1980s, the mandatory ban on interest on business checking accounts had remained. It is now history.

The Not-So-Good Things in Dodd-Frank

Although Dodd-Frank has some beneficial components, it neglected to resolve several key issues that were related to the financial crisis and overreached in some areas.

Silence on Fannie and Freddie. The two large government-sponsored enterprises (GSEs)—Fannie Mae and Freddie Mac—contributed to the housing boom. Although nominally the GSEs are publicly traded corporations, both companies had enough special ties to, and special favors from, the federal government that the financial markets considered their liabilities to carry an implicit government guarantee. This gave the GSEs a further advantage in the form of cheaper financing costs. As major investors in and securitizers and guarantors of residential mortgages, the two GSEs together owned or guaranteed about 40 percent of all mortgages in the run-up to the crisis.

Starting in the late 1990s and accelerating after 2003, the two GSEs lowered their lending standards. As a result, the mortgages in which they were investing or that they were guaranteeing became increasingly risky, but their (excessively low) capital levels did not adjust commensurately. As defaults and concomitant losses mounted after mid-2006, the GSEs' financial situation became increasingly shaky. At the same time, their share of new mortgage originations was increasing as the post-2006 losses on MBS decimated the private-label securitization market. By late summer 2008 they were clearly insolvent, and the federal government placed them in conservatorships in early September 2008. As a consequence, they continue to operate. They have even expanded their operations and recently have accounted for 60–70 percent of new mortgage originations. If the Federal Housing Administration (FHA), which also insures mortgages and is within the US Department of Housing and Urban Development, is included, government-supported entities currently account for over 90 percent of new mortgage originations.

Although few policymakers profess a belief that Fannie and Freddie should continue to operate at the center of the mortgage markets, Dodd-Frank was silent with respect to any specific actions for the GSEs' future, other than to mandate a report by the Obama administration (which it delivered in February 2011).

Unfortunately, this lack of action was a harbinger. Over two years later there has still been no congressional action with respect to the GSEs, and none is likely until well after the November 2012 election. The future structure of residential finance in the United States continues to hang in limbo.

The Volcker Rule. Dodd-Frank includes a prohibition—originally proposed by former Federal Reserve chairman Paul Volcker—on proprietary trading of financial instruments by banks (and their affiliates) and on banks' ownership of hedge funds. Some critics of the financial sector believe the elimination of the 1930s separation (embodied in the Glass-Steagall Act of 1933) of commercial banking and investment banking by the Gramm-Leach-Bliley Act of 1999 and the "deregulation" that followed were responsible for the crisis. The Volcker Rule was seen as a symbolic halfway resurrection of the Glass-Steagall boundary.

Unfortunately, in addition to being extremely difficult to implement, the Volcker Rule is unnecessary. Proprietary trading did not cause the financial crisis and neither did banks' ownership of hedge funds.

A far better, and more principled, approach would have been to establish the following rule: A bank (or a SIFI) can engage in any activity that is "examinable and supervisable" (E&S)—an activity for which bank regulators can establish appropriate capital requirements (meaning the risks are understood) and can make reasoned assessments of whether a bank is managing the activity well (that is, execution risks are not being added to the underlying risks of the activity). Since capital requirements and managerial assessments are at the heart of modern prudential regulation—how could prudential regulators allow a financial institution to engage in an activity for which capital requirements cannot be determined or managerial assessments cannot be made?—an E&S approach would be in harmony with modern prudential regulation. Only non-E&S activities would be banned from the bank or the SIFI (but such activities could still be allowable for a bank holding company that is not a SIFI).

Increased Regulation of Credit Rating Agencies. Despite Dodd-Frank's efforts to reduce regulatory reliance on credit rating agencies, the act expands the SEC's regulation of the special category of rating agencies—nationally recognized statistical rating organizations (NRSROs)—that the SEC created in 1975 and that includes the major three rating agencies (Moody's, Standard & Poor's, and Fitch) plus six smaller firms. The act directs the SEC to require the NRSROs to address conflict-of-interest problems (especially an issue for the major agencies, which have a business model whereby the issuer of the bonds that are being rated pays the fees for the rating) and transparency of information issues.

Unfortunately, this type of regulation will raise the costs of being an NRSRO and will thereby discourage entry into the rating business while also making business more difficult for the smaller NRSROs because the increased regulatory costs will tend to be lumpy and fixed, rather than proportionate to size. Innovation in the rating business will likely suffer. Ironically, it may also make the three major rating agencies even more important than they already are.

In addition, Dodd-Frank expanded the liability exposure of all rating agencies, regardless of whether they are NRSROs. The goal, of course, is to make the rating agencies more careful in their assessments. The danger is that they might also become more cautious, thereby reducing the amount of useful information they provide. Again, the burden may fall more heavily on smaller agencies.

A Freeze on Industrial Loan Companies. Industrial loan companies (ILCs) are depository institutions with state charters in a few states—notably Utah—that (unlike virtually all banks) can be owned by companies that are not financial institutions (for example, BMW, Toyota, and Pitney Bowes own ILCs). An ILC must obtain deposit insurance from the FDIC before it can use its charter and open its doors to customers.

Dodd-Frank placed a three-year moratorium on the FDIC's granting of deposit insurance to newly chartered ILCs (or to ILCs for which charters have been transferred). Since ILCs played no role in the financial crisis, this is unnecessary. Instead, it is another manifestation of the belief that excessive "deregulation" in general somehow caused the crisis. The drawback is that potential entry by nonfinancial companies into the depository business has been delayed and possibly (if the moratorium is made permanent) thwarted.

The Regulation of Interchange Fees on Debit Cards. Interchange fees on debit cards are the fees that debit card networks (that is, Visa and MasterCard) transfer from the banks that deal with merchants to the banks that issue debit cards. These debit card networks played no role in the financial crisis. Nevertheless, the Durbin amendment in Dodd-Frank required the Federal Reserve to establish cost-based maximum interchange fees on the debit cards issued by large banks.

This type of price regulation is usually reserved for local public utility regulation of substantial local monopolies, such as electricity distribution, water distribution, and natural gas distribution. Although the interchange fees were unlikely to be the result of textbook-style perfect competition, neither would they appear to be in the same category as local electricity prices. The encouragement of entry, rather than the imposition of price regulation, would have been preferable.

The Absence of a Tax on Size. If the large size (as measured by assets) of a financial institution is considered a societal problem (say, because its size also generates potential systemic consequences), then the appropriate model for regulating it is the economists' paradigm of "negative externality." For this kind of negative externality, the best policy tool is a tax on size, which would be far preferable to the "command and control" approach of either limiting what large financial institutions can do or trying to break up large institutions arbitrarily.

Although the Obama administration proposed a tax on the size of large financial institutions in early 2009, the idea never gained traction and was not included in Dodd-Frank. This was a missed opportunity.

Conclusion

In an 849-page omnibus piece of legislation, there are bound to be some good things and some not-so-good things. I have provided the highlights of both categories.

Suppose one had the opportunity to accept or reject the act in its entirety. In that case, I would clench my teeth and vote to accept it. But I would strongly wish it was not such a close call. Better, of course, would be a set of future changes to Dodd-Frank that kept the good parts and repealed the not-so-good parts. Whether that is realistic I leave to others to judge.

A Missed Opportunity

The Paulson Plan as an Alternative Framework to Dodd-Frank

by J. W. Verret

OUR YEARS AGO the nation faced an unprecedented financial crisis. The stock market took a steep dive and leaders
seemed clueless as the regulatory-reform process stalled for
two years. For better or worse, the Paulson Treasury Department
was substantially ahead of the curve on financial regulatory reform
before it became a topic of household conversation during the election of 2008, and the financial regulation reforms passed in 2010.

Treasury Secretary Henry Paulson and Undersecretary Robert
K. Steel undertook their Blueprint for Financial Regulatory Reform
in 2007. They submitted their Blueprint in March 2008, six months
prior to the collapse of Lehman Brothers and prior to the fall of
Bear Stearns or AIG.[1] The blueprint represented a thoughtful set of
proposals to prepare for and prevent future financial crises. It was
remarkably prescient.

The project began when Paulson convened a panel of experts
to consider reforming financial markets in March 2007, when the

capital-market intermediation process still ticked like a handmade Swiss clock. Seven months later the Dow would hit its current record high of 13,930. Andrew Ross Sorkin's fascinating account of the 2008 bailout leads readers to believe the midnight oil at Treasury was first lit in 2008, but in fact it was lit a full year earlier.[2] However, Congress did not take up the recommendations or hold hearings on the blueprint. Hearings began only after the financial meltdown of September 2008, and the Dodd-Frank Wall Street Reform and Consumer Protection Act of 2010 passed two years later.

The Democratic Congress, however, did not consider the central proposals in the blueprint while crafting Dodd-Frank.[3] This essay takes the blueprint off the shelf and considers many of the substantive recommendations of that report, particularly as compared against the many areas in Dodd-Frank that represent a 180-degree turn from those recommendations. This essay will contrast the Paulson Blueprint, which predated and in many ways predicted the financial crisis of 2008, with Dodd-Frank, which was justified as a reaction to the crisis but falls short as a solution to that crisis.[4]

The goal is not necessarily to endorse any provision in the Paulson Blueprint, which is best described as a measured and balanced, but still government-centric, approach to financial market reform. The Paulson Blueprint nevertheless serves as a useful conceit to the Dodd-Frank Act. The Paulson Blueprint proposes a more Hayekian solution[5] premised on the benefits of spontaneous order, although free flows of information through markets may well be preferable to either approach. This essay compares Dodd-Frank to the Paulson Blueprint to offer perspective on how Dodd-Frank is an excessive and overly broad response to the financial crisis of 2008.

The Paulson Blueprint opened with a recommendation that the President's Working Group (PWG) on Financial Markets, a group that coordinates among the Treasury secretary, Federal Reserve chairman, Securities and Exchange Commission (SEC) chairman, and

Commodity Futures Trading Commission (CFTC) chairman, be modernized and expanded.[6] The PWG was created by executive order in response to the stock market crash of 1987 and was reviewed favorably by the Government Accountability Office (GAO).[7]

The Paulson Blueprint recommended giving the PWG a much broader agenda for the regulators from different agencies to discuss and coordinate the entire financial sector, rather than merely the financial markets, to reflect the modern and interconnected financial system. It suggested expanding the size of the group to include other banking agencies and focused the group's mission toward coordination and information-sharing across agencies. It did not, however, suggest that the authority of existing independent agencies be usurped.

In contrast, Dodd-Frank created the Financial Stability Oversight Council (FSOC).[8] The FSOC, chaired by the Treasury secretary, functions as a council of regulators.[9] On the FSOC, various regulators vote to determine whether a firm is systemically significant, even if the firm is of a type entirely different from those the regulators currently oversee at their own agency.[10] Thus, the FSOC has the power to designate nonbank financial institutions as too big to fail and subject them to extensive regulation by the Federal Reserve.[11] Though Paulson was the driving force behind the bailout of 2008, the Paulson Blueprint did not embrace bailouts as national policy as directly, or to the same extent, as Dodd-Frank does. Moreover, rather than serve as a coordination mechanism for interagency disputes, the FSOC has more frequently been described as a forum for turf battles between agencies.[12]

Some have blamed mortgage origination for causing the crisis, though that claim has a troublesome foundation.[13] Proceeding ad arguendo, there again Paulson was one step ahead of the game. The Paulson Blueprint offered a viable solution for regulating disclosure problems in the mortgage origination process.

er the Paulson Blueprint, a Federal Mortgage Origination sion would have rated the effectiveness of state licensing commissions, giving investors in mortgage-backed securities information they could use in pricing their investments.[14] Instead, Dodd-Frank set up a regulatory agency that has been alleged in court to violate the separation of powers principles of the US Constitution.[15]

The Paulson Blueprint recognized deficiencies in federal oversight of chartered institutions operating in the mortgage market and further noted the potential benefits of some federal coordination of the state-based system for mortgage origination to set minimum standards for a state licensing system for mortgage originators that would also keep track of disciplinary history.[16]

Dodd-Frank, on the other hand, created a regulatory agency unlike any other in the federal bureaucracy when it designed the Consumer Financial Protection Bureau (CFPB): In contrast to the measured approach of the Paulson Blueprint, Dodd-Frank designated a single director to lead an agency[17] with a nearly $500 million annual budget immune from congressional appropriation.[18] The president's removal power over the director is limited, as is judicial review of agency decisions. The CFPB director has the authority to designate nearly any credit practice, such as, for instance, frequent-flier miles, as "abusive" and therefore prohibited. There would be very little review of such a decision.

Many have blamed a lack of coherent divisions of authority between the SEC and CFTC for contributing to the crisis. The Paulson Blueprint suggested consolidating these two agencies long before anyone else focused on that problem. The SEC and CFTC were created separately during a time when derivatives were primarily agricultural and distinct from other financial products. Those hard distinctions have begun to blur as futures and stock exchanges consolidate and products begin to share attributes. These two separate regulatory agencies remain and continue to fight over turf that overlaps at times.

At a hearing in September 2011, in which this author testified, Representative Barney Frank openly admitted the importance of following the Paulson Blueprint's recommendation to consolidate these two agencies, and yet claimed he was powerless to do so despite leading the most significant legislative changes to the financial regulatory landscape since 1933 through Congress. He noted:

> Let me just say, my last point, as I read all the testimony—I may not be able to come back to Commissioner Atkins. He had one thing in there in which he talked about how much more logical it would be if we were—and better if we would be able to merge the SEC and CFTC, to which I can only say, I wish. If I was making a new country, there would be one such entity. But unfortunately, interests do vest.[19]

The Paulson Blueprint urged a merger of the CFTC and the SEC to provide for unified oversight of financial products like swaps that are treated differently as a result of bureaucratic turf wars but are essentially the same product.[20] Not only did Dodd-Frank fail to consolidate the existing agencies, but it also perpetuated the inefficient bifurcation of financial-product regulation by dividing jurisdiction in Title VII between swaps (given to the CFTC) and security-based swaps (given to the SEC).[21]

To minimize regulatory barriers to coordination, the Paulson Blueprint recommended a requirement that Federal Reserve regulators be permitted access to SEC and CFTC examination information and accompany SEC and CFTC examiners on inspections for institutions representing systemic concerns.[22] This would have been accomplished through information-sharing arrangements between the agencies and would not have risked too-big-to-fail designations or turf wars that have become endemic to the FSOC. The only area in which Dodd-Frank incorporated[23] a recommendation in the Paulson

Blueprint was in phasing out the Office of Thrift Supervision (OTS), which was universally accepted as a failed regulatory agency.[24] The Paulson Blueprint described how innovations in banking and credit made the thrift charter redundant and outdated. Many have since blamed OTS for the failure of AIG, since OTS was the primary regulator of its troubled divisions.[25] Paulson's report called for breaking up OTS six months before the fall of AIG, but Congress ignored his report when it was delivered. It took over two years, and the subsequent failure of AIG, for Congress to finally pass legislation implementing that recommendation.

Paulson is most known for the bailout of 2008 and the extraordinary departure from basic principles of market discipline it represented and the future moral-hazard problems it is likely to cause. Debate over the wisdom of the size, scope, and strategy of the bailout of 2008–2009, executed under Presidents Bush and Obama and Secretaries Paulson and Geithner, is likely to continue. In full disclosure, the author has been a vocal critic of the bailout begun under Paulson's tenure, particularly the decision to take equity investments in bailout recipients rather than use auction mechanisms for buying troubled assets.[26]

Credit must nonetheless be given where due. The Paulson Blueprint is not without its flaws, but the report was proactive and prescient. More importantly, when considered next to Dodd-Frank, it provides perspective for the overly broad and cumbersome changes implemented by Dodd-Frank. Messrs. Dodd and Frank failed to consider the Paulson Blueprint in their lawmaking, despite the fact that it actually predicted many of the events of the crisis.

NOTES

1. See Department of the Treasury, "Blueprint for a Modernized Financial Regulation Structure," March 2008, http://www.treasury.gov/press-center/press-releases /Documents/Blueprint.pdf.

2. See generally Andrew Ross Sorkin, *Too Big to Fail* (New York: Viking, 2009).

3. There are a handful of exceptions, such as the abolition of the Office of Thrift Supervision and the creation of a Federal Insurance Office in the Treasury with little actual authority. The central provisions of Department of the Treasury, "Blueprint for a Modernized Financial Regulation Structure," were nevertheless ignored.

4. For a more expansive critique of the Dodd-Frank Act, see Stephen M. Bainbridge, "Dodd-Frank: Quack Federal Corporate Governance Round II," *Minnesota Law Review* 95 (2011): 1779.

5. See generally Friedrich August von Hayek, "The Use of Knowledge in Society," *American Economic Review* 35, no. 4 (September 1945): 519–30.

6. See Department of the Treasury, "Blueprint for a Modernized Financial Regulation Structure," 75.

7. See GAO, "Financial Regulatory Coordination: The Role and Functioning of the President's Working Group" (GGD-00-46, Washington, DC, January 21, 2000).

8. *Dodd-Frank Wall Street Reform and Consumer Protection Act*, Public Law 111-203, *U.S. Statutes at Large* 124 (2010), § 111.

9. Ibid.

10. Ibid., § 112.

11. Ibid., § 113.

12. See, for example, Damian Paletta, "Infighting Besets Financial-Oversight Council," *Wall Street Journal*, September 29, 2010.

13. See, for example, Todd Zywicki, "In Elizabeth Warren We Trust?" *Wall Street Journal*, September 30, 2010.

14. See Department of the Treasury, "Blueprint for a Modernized Financial Regulation Structure," 6–7.

15. See J. W. Verret, "About the Dodd-Frank Act, George Washington Would Be Turning Over in His Grave," *Forbes*, July 2, 2012, http://www.forbes.com/sites/real spin/2012/07/02/about-the-dodd-frank-act-george-washington-would-be-turning -over-in-his-grave.

16. See Department of the Treasury, "Blueprint for a Modernized Financial Regulation Structure," 78.

17. *Dodd-Frank Wall Street Reform and Consumer Protection Act*, § 1011(b).

18. Ibid., § 1017(a)(2).

19. House Committee on Financial Services, *Fixing the Watchdog: Legislative Proposals to Improve and Enhance the Securities and Exchange Commission*, 112th Cong., 1st sess. (September 15, 2011), 17, http://financialservices.house.gov/uploadedfiles/112-62.pdf.

20. See Department of the Treasury, "Blueprint for a Modernized Financial Regulation Structure," 11–13.

21. *Dodd-Frank Wall Street Reform and Consumer Protection Act*, § 712.

22. See Department of the Treasury, "Blueprint for a Modernized Financial Regulation Structure," 85.

23. *Dodd-Frank Wall Street Reform and Consumer Protection Act*, §§ 312 and 313.

24. See Department of the Treasury, "Blueprint for a Modernized Financial Regulation Structure," 89.

25. See, for example, Chana Joffe-Walt, "Regulating AIG: Who Fell Asleep on the Job?" National Public Radio, June 5, 2009, http://www.npr.org/templates/story/story.php?storyId=104979546.

26. See generally J. W. Verret, "Treasury Inc.: How the Bailout Reshapes Corporate Theory and Practice," *Yale Journal on Regulation* 27, no. 2 (2010): 283–350.

Quantifying and Projecting Dodd-Frank's Provisions

by Patrick A. McLaughlin and Robert W. Greene

T HE DODD-FRANK WALL Street Reform and Consumer Protection Act of 2010 (Dodd-Frank) was signed into law July 21, 2010.[1] The act requires the creation—by one count—of 398 new rules,[2] and will affect the US economy by restricting or requiring specific activities. Until recently, no method existed by which to measure comprehensively the number of restrictions imposed upon an economy by a specific legislative act such as Dodd-Frank. In this analysis, we use the methodology of RegData, developed by Patrick A. McLaughlin and Omar Al-Ubaydli at the Mercatus Center at George Mason University, to quantify objectively the number of new restrictions Dodd-Frank created via rules adopted through the end of 2011.[3] We estimate that Dodd-Frank generated 2,109 new restrictions within Title 12 (Banks and Banking) and Title 17 (Commodity and Securities Exchanges) of the Code of Federal Regulations (CFR) by the end of 2011.[4] If the number of restrictions created by each new Dodd-Frank rule continues at this rate, Dodd-Frank will cause a 26 percent increase in the restrictions within CFR Titles 12 and 17 once all Dodd-Frank rulemakings are finalized.

Methodology

RegData quantifies the impact of regulations based on the actual content of the CFR. In other words, RegData relies on the content of regulatory text as a data source. RegData parses the CFR to count the number of binding constraints—words that indicate an obligation to comply, such as "shall" or "must"—published in the CFR. We adopt the RegData method to quantify Dodd-Frank rulemakings completed through 2011 as a way of assessing the act's impact and to give perspective on its scale relative to previously existing regulations.

To identify the rules finalized pursuant to Dodd-Frank authority between the date Dodd-Frank became law and December 31, 2011, we used a publicly available list of final Dodd-Frank rules and notices compiled by the Federal Reserve Bank of St. Louis.[5] According to this list, 63 of Dodd-Frank's required or permitted rulemakings had been published as final rules by the end of 2011.[6]

The RegData method uses regulatory text from the CFR. Because the 2013 CFR, which will include Dodd-Frank rulemakings promulgated during 2012, has yet to be published, this analysis is limited to new restrictions generated by the 63 Dodd-Frank rulemakings finalized by December 31, 2011, as compiled by the Federal Reserve Bank of St. Louis.

Guidance documents and other similar agency or agency staff documents that do not modify the CFR may nevertheless impose actual or de facto restrictions. The RegData method does not account for these restrictions because they are not included in the CFR. Additionally, certain Dodd-Frank rules were not included in the Federal Reserve Bank of St. Louis list.[7] Therefore, our analysis likely understates the number of new restrictions Dodd-Frank has generated.

To use the RegData method to calculate the number of restrictions Dodd-Frank created through 2011, we first identified the parts of the 2010 and 2011 CFRs that were newly created, altered, or amended by each of the 63 Dodd-Frank rules finalized in 2010 or 2011.[8] If only one part of the CFR was affected, we compared the number of restrictions in the amended part with the number of restrictions in the part prior to amendment. For example, if a rule was finalized in 2010, we compared the number of restrictions in the affected part of the 2011 CFR with the same part of the 2010 CFR, which had been printed before the rule existed. The difference in restrictions served as our estimate of the number of restrictions generated by that particular Dodd-Frank rule.[9] If a rule added an entirely new part to the CFR, we used the RegData method to calculate the number of restrictions in that new part and, hence, the number of restrictions attributable to the new rule.

As an example, according to our analysis, the Federal Deposit Insurance Corporation's July 12, 2011, rule on retail foreign exchange transactions created 115 new restrictions.[10] To reach this figure, we first identified which parts of the CFR were amended by the retail foreign exchange transactions rule. The final rule's preamble, published in the *Federal Register,* states that it only affects 12 CFR Part 349. We then compared the number of restrictions in 12 CFR Part 349 of 2011 to the number of restrictions in 12 CFR Part 349 of 2012. Because no other 2010 or 2011 Dodd-Frank rule impacts 12 CFR Part 349 and because no other part of the CFR was affected by the retail foreign exchange transactions rule, we were able to estimate that the rule created 115 new restrictions.[11]

If a final rule newly created, altered, or amended multiple parts of the CFR, the methodology included an additional step. After identifying which parts of the CFR a particular rule changed, we calculated the number of restrictions within each affected part before and after the rule was finalized. The difference reflected the number of restrictions added to each part by the particular rule. To obtain the total number of restrictions added by a rule, we summed the number of restrictions for all affected parts of the CFR to get the total number of restrictions added by the particular rule.

To calculate the total quantity of new restrictions created by Dodd-Frank rules in 2010 and 2011, we applied the above methodology to the 63 final rules taken from the list compiled by the Federal Reserve Bank of St. Louis. We then summed the number of restrictions generated by the 63 rules. To prevent overestimation, in which one part of the CFR was affected by multiple Dodd-Frank rules, we subtracted all duplicates from our total. Thus, the changes to each affected part of the CFR were counted only once. This approach ensured that we counted restrictions added to particular parts of the CFR by 2010 and 2011 Dodd-Frank rules only once, even if multiple Dodd-Frank rules affected the same parts.

Findings

Using this methodology, we estimate that between July 21, 2010 (when Dodd-Frank became law) and December 31, 2011, Dodd-Frank led to the addition of 2,109 new restrictions to titles 12 and 17 of the CFR. That represents an 8.2 percent increase from the 25,703 restrictions that existed in the modified parts before Dodd-Frank altered or amended them.

It is important to bear in mind, however, that many of Dodd-Frank's most substantial rulemakings have yet to be finalized. While this analysis has only considered the 63 rules listed as finalized prior to the end of 2011, Dodd-Frank requires the creation of—by one count—a total of 398 regulations.[12] Assuming the remaining regulations are proportionately restrictive—that is, assuming they contain a similar number of restrictions per regulation as the 63 considered in this analysis—Dodd-Frank would create 13,323 new restrictions in total. To give this figure—13,323—additional perspective, we compared it to the total number of restrictions in effect in 2010 in titles

12 and 17 of the CFR, in which many federal financial regulations are published. In 2010, titles 12 and 17 contained a total of 51,116 restrictions. If Dodd-Frank adds 13,323 restrictions to those CFR titles, it will have caused a 26 percent increase in restrictions in those titles.

These results are consistent with our expectations that Dodd-Frank, by expanding the regulatory framework into new areas and creating new categories of registrants, would add a large number of new regulatory requirements.

We separately examined which parts of the CFR have experienced the largest increase in restrictions during 2010 and 2011 as a result of Dodd-Frank. These are listed in Table 1.

These parts of the CFR house key pieces of new regulatory frameworks established by Dodd-Frank. Accordingly, the large number of restrictions is consistent with our expectations. The Commodity Futures Trading Commission's (CFTC's) 2010 final rule on off-exchange retail foreign exchange transactions and intermediaries is responsible for the large increase in restrictions within 17 CFR 5, "Off-Exchange Foreign Currency Transactions."[13] Two 2011 CFTC rules are responsible for the significant increase in restrictions to 17

Table 1. The Four CFR Parts with the Most New Dodd-Frank Restrictions

Title	Part	Number of New Restrictions	Agency
17	5	306	Commodity Futures Trading Commission
17	39	272	Commodity Futures Trading Commission
17	49	262	Commodity Futures Trading Commission
17	240	152	Securities and Exchange Commission

Source: Authors' calculations.

CFR 39, "Derivatives Clearing Organizations."[14] These rules are components of the new regulatory regime for over-the-counter derivatives, a central element of Dodd-Frank. The restrictions added to Part 49 of Title 17, "Swap Data Repositories," by a 2011 CFTC final rule are also part of the new derivatives regime.[15] The increase in restrictions within 17 CFR 240, "General Rules and Regulations, Securities Exchange Act of 1934," is the result of several new Securities and Exchange Commission rules, including the commission's 2011 final rule establishing a new whistleblower program.[16]

Conclusion

In this analysis, we have adapted the method of quantifying regulations pioneered by RegData to estimate the total number of new restrictions Dodd-Frank created in the regulatory text. Because the 2013 CFR has yet to be published, our analysis is limited to only 63 final rules identified by the Federal Reserve Bank of St. Louis as resulting from Dodd-Frank by December 31, 2011. We estimate that over that period Dodd-Frank created 2,109 new restrictions. If subsequent Dodd-Frank rules are proportionately restrictive—that is to say, if the number of restrictions per Dodd-Frank rule remains the same as the ratio for rules finalized between 2010 and 2011—Dodd-Frank will add a total of 13,323 new restrictions to CFR titles 12 and 17, where most financial regulations are codified. If this number of new restrictions is added to those titles, Dodd-Frank will cause a 26 percent increase in the number of restrictions in CFR titles 12 and 17 when compared to restrictions in those titles in 2010.

Of course, the new rules could be more or less restrictive than the rules adopted through the end of 2011. Many of the central and most complex rulemakings under Dodd-Frank have yet to be finalized. Once the 2013 CFR is available, we will be able to analyze 2012 rules.

As more rules are finalized in 2013 and beyond, we plan to continue to analyze them using the RegData method.

NOTES

1. *Dodd-Frank Wall Street Reform and Consumer Protection Act*, Public Law 111-203, *U.S. Statutes at Large* 124 (2010).

2. Davis Polk, "Dodd-Frank Progress Report," Davis Polk Regulatory Tracker, November 2012, 2, http://www.davispolk.com/files/Publication/9a990de9-911b-4e6b-b183-08b071d8b008/Presentation/PublicationAttachment/8363256a-524d-4d65-8ebe-096127dab2a3/Nov2012_Dodd.Frank.Progress.Report.pdf.

3. To learn more about the methodology behind RegData, see Omar Al-Ubaydli and Patrick McLaughlin, "RegData: The Industry-Specific Regulatory Constraint Database," Mercatus Center at George Mason University, October 15, 2012, http://mercatus.org/publication/industry-specific-regulatory-constraint-database-ircd. For another overview of the methodology behind RegData, see Mercatus Center at George Mason University, "RegData Methodology," http://regdata.mercatus.org/about. Because Dodd-Frank rulemaking is ongoing, the estimate of restrictions created through the end of 2011 does not measure the total effect of the act. Rather, the estimate comprehensively measures only restrictions in rules finalized by December 31, 2011. Many of the most significant rulemakings have yet to be finalized.

4. All rules examined in this analysis affect only Titles 12 and 17, and most future rulemakings caused by Dodd-Frank are expected primarily to affect only those titles.

5. "Dodd-Frank Regulatory Reform Rules: Final Rules and Notices," Federal Reserve Bank of St. Louis, http://www.stlouisfed.org/regreformrules/final.aspx.

6. Ibid. For the purposes of this analysis, we omit final notices, temporary modifications, and rules pertaining to administrative procedure or agency reorganization. Omitting these items gives us our figure of 63 rules finalized pursuant to Dodd-Frank authority between the date Dodd-Frank became law and December 31, 2011. We omitted items that do not amend existing CFR text because they cannot be analyzed using the RegData method, which relies exclusively on CFR text. We omitted rules pertaining to agency administration or reorganization because they would have artificially inflated our results with restrictions that exclusively affect government administration.

7. See, for example, "Minority and Women Inclusion, Final Rule," *Federal Register* 75 (December 28, 2010), 81395; and "Facilitating Shareholder Direct Nominations, Final Rule," *Federal Register* 75 (September 16, 2010), 56667. Neither of these rules,

although promulgated under Dodd-Frank, is included in the list compiled by the Federal Reserve Bank of St. Louis.

8. To identify which CFR parts were created, altered, or amended by each of the 63 Dodd-Frank rules finalized in 2010 and 2011, we examined the *Federal Register* notice published for each of these final rules. Each final rule notice in the *Federal Register* lists all CFR parts affected by that particular final rule. Using this information, we created a database listing the CFR parts affected by each final rule. This database enabled us to determine which parts of the CFR were affected by Dodd-Frank rules finalized in 2010 and 2011, and how many of these parts were affected by multiple rules.

9. Because it is possible that other rules unrelated to Dodd-Frank also affected the same CFR parts, we emphasize that this is an estimate rather than an exact figure.

10. "Retail Foreign Exchange Transactions, Final Rule," *Federal Register* 76, (July 12, 2011), 40779.

11. A search of the 2011 *Federal Register* yielded no simultaneous alterations or amendments to 12 CFR Part 349 during 2011. For other rules, however, we cannot say with certainty that no other rule unrelated to Dodd-Frank simultaneously altered or amended relevant parts of the CFR.

12. Davis Polk, "Dodd-Frank Progress Report," 2.

13. "Regulation of Off-Exchange Retail Foreign Exchange Transactions and Intermediaries, Final Rule," *Federal Register* 75 (September 10, 2010), 55410.

14. "Process for Review of Swaps and Mandatory Clearing, Final Rule," *Federal Register* 76 (July 26, 2011), 44464; and "Derivatives Clearing Organization General Provisions and Core Principles, Final Rule," *Federal Register* 76 (November 8, 2011), 89333.

15. "Swap Data Repositories: Registration Standards, Duties and Core Principles, Final Rule," *Federal Register* 76 (September 1, 2011), 54538.

16. "Securities Whistleblower Incentives and Protections, Final Rule," *Federal Register* 76 (June 13, 2011), 34300.

Conclusion

by Hester Peirce and James Broughel

T HIS BOOK PAINTS a fairly bleak picture of Dodd-Frank. Dodd-Frank was presented as a solution to the devastating problems that emerged in 2007 and 2008. It is not that. Certain elements did not relate to the crisis at all. Other provisions could make the financial system more prone to crises.

The natural question is, what should we have done? A comprehensive alternative solution is beyond the scope of this book, but any response to the crisis should have included the following twelve elements. Dodd-Frank ignored most of these elements, and the few it included were not crafted with the necessary deliberative care.

1. The housing finance system should be reshaped to diminish the role of the federal government and the US taxpayer.
2. The regulatory structure for financial institutions should be revisited with a reduced role for the Federal Reserve—which should focus on its weighty monetary-policy responsibilities—and clearer lines of accountability than the current diffuse regulatory structure allows.
3. A merger of the SEC and CFTC should be considered in response to their increasingly overlapping jurisdictions.
4. Improvements should be made to the manner in which over-the-counter derivatives are recorded and reported to regulators.

5. The bankruptcy code should be revised to make it more credible as a tool for handling failed financial institutions.

6. Measures should be taken to increase shareholders' and creditors' incentives to monitor and constrain the risk of financial institutions, such as a reduction in deposit insurance, double liability for shareholders, and contingent capital schemes.

7. Greater constraints should be placed on the design of and accountability for emergency government-rescue programs.

8. There should be increased disclosure with respect to the underlying assets in securitization pools.

9. Statutory and regulatory mandates to rely on credit ratings should be eliminated.

10. Money market fund regulation should be revisited in light of events during 2008.

11. The repurchase and securities lending markets should be addressed in light of their role in the recent crisis.

12. Finally, a simpler approach to capital regulation should be considered, including the propriety of using risk weights in capital requirements.

These elements of a potential regulatory reform alternative to Dodd-Frank are broad ideas in need of careful consideration, analysis, and development. Dodd-Frank attempted some of these reforms, but, as discussed above, its approach was often flawed. As further steps are taken to understand the factors that contributed to the crisis, additional reform ideas are likely to emerge. The key theme in any financial regulatory reform should be increasing the incentive for market participants to monitor the financial system, a task which regulators, no matter how intelligent and hardworking, cannot carry out on their own.

Further Reading

For those interested in monitoring Dodd-Frank implementation or looking at Dodd-Frank in greater depth, the following is a list of useful sources. The views reflected in these pieces do not necessarily reflect the views of the authors of this book.

The text of Dodd-Frank is available at http://www.gpo.gov/fdsys/pkg /PLAW-111publ203/pdf/PLAW-111publ203.pdf.

For those who would prefer an abridged version, many law firms published summaries. Here are several helpful ones:

- Cleary Gottlieb, "Dodd-Frank Wall Street Reform and Consumer Protection Act Poised to Usher in Sweeping Reform of U.S. Financial Services Regulation," Alert Memo, July 9, 2010, http://www.cgsh.com /files/News/8a4361fa-131b-46b9-a3ad-779430dac8a6/Presentation /NewsAttachment/153327b9-3da0-4d63-b2cb-32c8022d8159/Cleary%20 Gottlieb%20Dodd-Frank%20Alert%20Memo.pdf.
- Davis Polk & Wardwell LLP, "Summary of the Dodd-Frank Wall Street Reform and Consumer Protection Act, Enacted into Law on July 21, 2010," July 21, 2010, http://www.davispolk.com/files /Publication/7084f9fe-6580-413b-b870-b7c025ed2ecf/Presenta tion/PublicationAttachment/1d4495c7-0be0-4e9a-ba77-f786f b90464a/070910_Financial_Reform_Summary.pdf.
- Debevoise and Plimpton, "Dodd-Frank Wall Street Reform and Consumer Protection Act: Summary of Key Provisions," June 30, 2010, http:// www.debevoise.com/publications/DoddFrankAct.pdf.

The following resources are useful for tracking Dodd-Frank Rulemaking:

- The Federal Reserve Bank of St. Louis tracks Dodd-Frank rulemaking. The tracker is available at http://www.stlouisfed.org/regreformrules.
- The law firm Davis Polk publishes quarterly Dodd-Frank progress reports on Dodd-Frank implementation. The reports are broken down by regulator and stage of rulemaking. The reports are available at http:// www.davispolk.com/Dodd-Frank-Rulemaking-Progress-Report/.

- The law firm Sullivan & Cromwell LLP has a searchable website, "Dodd-Frank Developments," that allows one to search by date, agency, and section. It is available at http://www.sullcrom.com/doddfrankdevelopments.

The following analyses of Dodd-Frank are useful for those who want to look a little deeper:

- Viral V. Acharya and M. Richardson, eds., *Regulating Wall Street: The Dodd-Frank Act and the New Architecture of Global Finance* (Hoboken, NJ: John Wiley and Sons, 2011).
- "The Dodd-Frank Act: Too Big Not to Fail," *The Economist,* February 18, 2012, http://www.economist.com/node/21547784/.
- David A. Skeel, *The New Financial Deal: Understanding the Dodd-Frank Act and Its (Unintended) Consequences* (Hoboken, NJ: John Wiley and Sons, 2011).

About the Authors

Hester Peirce is a senior research fellow at the Mercatus Center at George Mason University. Before joining Mercatus, she served as a senior counsel to the Republican staff on the Senate Committee on Banking, Housing, and Urban Affairs. Before that, she served as counsel to Commissioner Paul S. Atkins at the Securities and Exchange Commission and as a staff attorney in the Division of Investment Management at the Securities and Exchange Commission. She earned her BA in economics from Case Western Reserve University and her JD from Yale Law School.

James Broughel is the program manager of the Regulatory Studies Program at the Mercatus Center at George Mason University. He is a doctoral student in the economics program at George Mason University. He earned his MA in economics from Hunter College of the City University of New York.

Robert W. Greene is a research associate at the Mercatus Center at George Mason University. His research focuses on financial regulations, the regulatory process, and labor markets. Before joining Mercatus, Greene had served as a Governor's Fellow in Virginia's Office of the Secretary of Commerce and Trade. He holds a BBA in finance and public policy from the College of William and Mary.

Patrick A. McLaughlin is a senior research fellow at the Mercatus Center at George Mason University. He is the cofounder of RegData with economist Omar Al-Ubaydli. His research focuses on regulations and the regulatory process, and he has published peer-reviewed articles on administrative law, regulatory economics, law and economics, public choice, environmental economics, and international trade. Before joining Mercatus, McLaughlin served as a senior economist at the Federal Railroad Administration in the US Department of Transportation. He holds a PhD in economics from Clemson University.

J. W. Verret is an assistant professor at the George Mason University School of Law and a member of the Financial Markets Working Group at the Mercatus Center at George Mason University. His primary research interests include corporate governance, securities regulation, and executive compensation. He received his MA in public policy from the Harvard Kennedy School of Government and his JD from Harvard Law School.

Lawrence J. White is Robert Kavesh Professor of Economics at New York University's Stern School of Business and a Member of the Financial Markets Working Group at the Mercatus Center at George Mason University. From 1986 to 1989, he served as a board member at the Federal Home Loan Bank Board, in which capacity he also served as a board member for Freddie Mac. From 1982 to 1983, he served as the director of the Economic Policy Office, Antitrust Division, at the US Department of Justice. Professor White received his BA from Harvard University, his MSc from the London School of Economics, and his PhD from Harvard University.

Acknowledgment

The editors gratefully acknowledge the research assistance provided by Robert W. Greene.

Index

Page numbers in *italics* indicate tables; the letter n following a page number indicates a note; the letter t indicates a table.

25093121R00126

Made in the USA
Charleston, SC
16 December 2013